Forensic Pathology Case Studies

Forensic Pathology Case Studies

Edda Emanuela Guareschi
Medical, Molecular and Forensic Sciences,
College of Science, Health, Engineering and Education,
Murdoch University, Murdoch, WA, Australia

ELSEVIER
ACADEMIC PRESS
An imprint of Elsevier

Academic Press is an imprint of Elsevier
125 London Wall, London EC2Y 5AS, United Kingdom
525 B Street, Suite 1650, San Diego, CA 92101, United States
50 Hampshire Street, 5th Floor, Cambridge, MA 02139, United States
The Boulevard, Langford Lane, Kidlington, Oxford OX5 1GB, United Kingdom

Notices
Knowledge and best practice in this field are constantly changing. As new research and experience broaden our understanding, changes in research methods, professional practices, or medical treatment may become necessary.

Practitioners and researchers must always rely on their own experience and knowledge in evaluating and using any information, methods, compounds, or experiments described herein. In using such information or methods they should be mindful of their own safety and the safety of others, including parties for whom they have a professional responsibility.

To the fullest extent of the law, neither the Publisher nor the authors, contributors, or editors, assume any liability for any injury and/or damage to persons or property as a matter of products liability, negligence or otherwise, or from any use or operation of any methods, products, instructions, or ideas contained in the material herein.

British Library Cataloguing-in-Publication Data
A catalogue record for this book is available from the British Library

Library of Congress Cataloging-in-Publication Data
A catalog record for this book is available from the Library of Congress

ISBN: 978-0-12-824294-0

For Information on all Academic Press publications
visit our website at https://www.elsevier.com/books-and-journals

Publisher: Stacy Masucci
Acquisitions Editor: Elizabeth Brown
Editorial Project Manager: Mariana L. Kuhl
Production Project Manager: Kiruthika Govindaraju
Cover Designer: Mark Rogers

Typeset by MPS Limited, Chennai, India

CONTENTS

LIST OF CONTRIBUTORS

Letizia Gnetti
S.C. Anatomia e istologia patologica, Azienda Ospedaliero-Universitaria di Parma, Parma, Italy

Edda Emanuela Guareschi
Medical, Molecular and Forensic Sciences, College of Science, Health, Engineering and Education, Murdoch University, Murdoch, WA, Australia

Paola Annarosa Magni
Medical, Molecular and Forensic Sciences, College of Science, Health, Engineering and Education, Murdoch University, Murdoch, WA, Australia; Murdoch University Singapore, Singapore

Maria Laura Schirripa
Dipartimento di Medicina e Chirurgia, Universita' di Parma, Parma, Italy

ABOUT THE EDITOR

Edda Emanuela Guareschi was born in Parma (Italy) and lives in Perth (Western Australia), with a husband and four cats. After graduating from Medicine School at the University of Bologna, she specialized in Forensic Pathology and Legal Medicine, and completed a Master of Science in Forensic Anthropology and Odontology at the University of Milan. Between 1998 and 2017, she worked as a forensic pathologist and anthropologist in northern Italy, and while acquiring an extensive professional casework, she has always updated her knowledge and skills by international training and by continuing to collaborate with academia through lectures, publications and conducting presentations in conferences all over the world. Since March 2018, she has been an Adjunct Lecturer in Forensic Science at Murdoch University, Western Australia, and in 2019, she started a PhD program studying forensic taphonomy in aquatic environments. Other research interests include Forensic Imaging, Pathology, Toxicology and Veterinary.

PREFACE

The Italian legal system is based on civil law and it is inquisitorial, as opposed to the Anglo-American common law legal system, which is adversarial. In the former, an extensive official investigation is performed before trial, whereas in the latter a competitive process between prosecution and defence takes place to determine the facts. These different legal systems impact the ways in which criminal cases are investigated and prosecuted.

In Italy, forensic pathologists are directly appointed by public prosecutors in the pretrial investigation, and their task is to ascertain time, cause, mode and manner of death of a deceased person. If the manner of death is natural, forensic pathologists are called to explain why death occurred by determining the correct clinical diagnosis of the deceased. In this case, the expertise of forensic pathologists overlaps with the one of anatomical/clinical pathologists, whose collaboration is extremely important but unfortunately not often achieved for several reasons. While unnatural deaths are basically attributable to homicide, suicide, accident and, in some cases, undetermined causes, clinical diagnoses leading to natural deaths can be attributable to thousands of pathological conditions. Therefore, natural deaths may be sometimes much more difficult to clarify than unnatural ones, especially if ante mortem history and/or clinical documentation are absent or unreliable. Forensic pathologists working in small cities deal with many more variable natural deaths than unnatural deaths. This variation in natural deaths can be stressful to deal with, for example if the cause of death is particularly rare and difficult to establish, or if medical malpractice is suspected.

After graduating from medicine school, I completed four years of training as a specialist forensic pathologist and entered into a professional career in Parma, the city in the north of Italy where I was born, went to high school and lived until recently. There, I was on a weekly roster in the forensic section of the local university hospital for 15 years. In the beginning, during the early 2000s, there was no forensic anthropologist to assist with skeletal or unrecognizable remains, which have although ever amounted to a few cases per year, so I took on the challenge to become a forensic anthropologist. Being both a forensic pathologist and anthropologist turned my reasonably quiet routine into a pretty unpredictable one, where I not only handled my assigned caseload, but was also called to consult for my fellow colleagues, both in Parma and in similar small towns of the surrounding northeast regions. The cases outlined in this book have been selected from my 15 years of casework, and can be rightfully described as unusual and/or intriguing. They come from different Italian cities and regions, and nearly all needed both deep reasoning and a wide range of expertise to be solved.

The last chapter deals with peculiar findings when imaging is applied to bodies in forensic cases, and highlights how the same imaging should become a crucial subject in both forensic higher education and investigations worldwide, following a new millennium trend already well established in metropolitan realities.

In the end, my professional experience, which I still regard as an adventure, has convinced me that working as a forensic pathologist in one's hometown can be rather unsettling. One's personal life, associated with personal history and memories, mixes and interferes far too often with one's working life. Documents, stories, work-related facts and people are a constant reminder of who one is and where one's origins lie. Sometimes this makes the strict scientific approach to the job quite difficult. Most pathologists are "normal" people who enjoy the simple things in life; therefore, they have to make a big effort to maintain a healthy mental balance when presented with the squalor, sadness and horrors of their job. I remember being summoned to violent crime scene investigations while I was spending some well-deserved time with my family on a sunny spring day, and all the relief and joy I had been feeling instantly vanished and were substituted by a stomach-churning anxiety. I regret the time I did not spend with my dog Zoe, now long gone, and I often meditate on the cynical fate of some dead people I have had to examine. Some of these were young, healthy and beautiful with a full life ahead of them, some old and forgotten, some just people I knew. I hope that both my present colleagues and the new generations of forensic pathologists, as readers, will share my thoughts and feelings, and will perpetuate their sincere commitment to a unique profession.

ACKNOWLEDGEMENTS

In addition to all the colleagues and experts who, at different times, were actively involved in the cases in the pursue of justice, I would like to thank Prof. Ian Dadour and Prof. John Watling for their constructive criticism and their assistance in my dealing with the tricks of the English language. Murdoch University colleagues Associate Prof. Philip Nicholls and Dr. Shanan Tobe need to be recognized, as well, for their constant confidence, encouragement and advice. I would also like to thank my husband, Alberto, for his patience and support during my professional years, when numerous evenings, a few nights and an unnerving number of weekends were lost to my job.

SECTION 1

Casework of Forensic Pathology

CHAPTER 1

The hermit and the street character: unusual diagnoses in forensic pathology

Edda Emanuela Guareschi
Medical, Molecular and Forensic Sciences, College of Science, Health, Engineering and Education, Murdoch University, Murdoch, WA, Australia

ABSTRACT
Two natural and unusual causes of death are depicted in this chapter, both regarding adult women living in peculiar social settings. In the forensic pathologist's routine natural deaths can, sometimes, be more difficult to determine, and explain, than violent deaths, such as homicides, suicides and accidents. The first deceased was a 39 years old woman living alone in an old and isolated country house, whose death was determined at autopsy as a fulminant septic shock by a pelvic inflammatory disease (PID) connected to the intrauterine presence of a contraceptive device (IUD). In the second case, the cause of death of the 44 years old homeless and mentally disabled woman was revealed by histopathological findings, which not only contradicted the diagnosis on admission to the infective diseases ward of the city hospital, but were also inconsistent with both the diagnosis of the cause of death delivered by the treating clinicians and the report of the clinical pathologist appointed to perform the autopsy. The second case was further complicated by the request of the prosecutor to evaluate the possibility of medical malpractice on the part of the hospital's treating staff.

Keywords: Intrauterine device (IUD); pelvic inflammatory disease (PID); toxic shock syndrome (TSS); fungal pneumonia; *Candida* spp; *Aspergillus* spp; medical malpractice

On a chilly night in late Autumn 2010, huddled up in an isolated and run-down country house, a 39 years old woman, her dog probably lying at her feet, chatted on the phone with her partner until 01:00 a.m. Nobody then heard from her until the following afternoon, when the police had to force the door to get access to the house, free her barking dog and then discover her dead body

Forensic Pathology Case Studies. DOI: https://doi.org/10.1016/B978-0-12-824294-0.00001-7

in the bathroom. She was seated on the toilet bowl with her cell phone laying abandoned on the bathroom floor. An investigation was launched to determine time, cause, mode and manner of death, even though violence or foul play seemed unlikely to have happened. The house was in fact locked and no signs of a struggle were found on her body or anywhere else.

The following external examination could only hint at an unusual cause of death by indicating a long surgical scar on her back, (confirming a history of spinal surgery for severe scoliosis) and traces of bleeding in the perineal region. The autopsy I performed on a grey morning, as it is so common at that time of the year, rolled on without any critical findings, and as I went on working, both the looming spectre of an obscure autopsy and the hope to explain that death with toxicology began shaping up. The turning point in the autopsy came as a complete surprise. Following the removal of the pelvic organs, the endopelvic fascia, a system of connective tissue between bladder, urethra, vagina, uterus and the pelvic walls, revealed hemorragic infiltrations close to the uterus, the fallopian tubes and both ovaries. Once incised, the fallopian tubes and the ovaries showed a bilateral suppurative inflammation (Fig. 1.1). An intrauterine contraceptive device (IUD) was located within the uterus (Fig. 1.2).

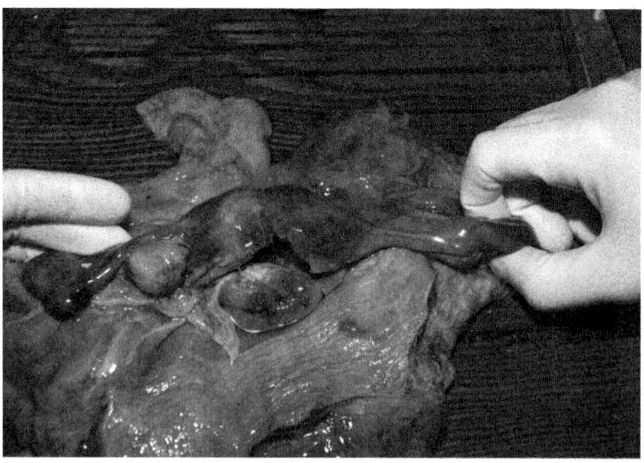

Figure 1.1 Bilateral suppurative inflammation of the fallopian tubes and the ovaries.

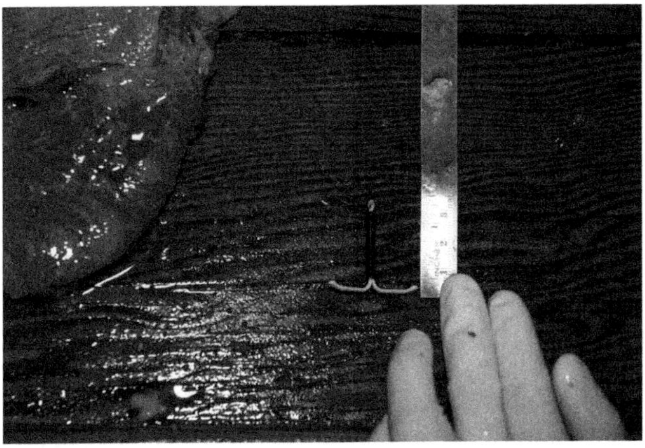

Figure 1.2 Intra-uterine contraceptive device.

Negative results from toxicology facilitated the diagnosis of the cause of death as septic shock associated with IUD-related pelvic inflammatory disease (PID).

The nosological existence of PID as a severe pelvic infection potentially leading to septic (also called toxic) shock has been reported in the clinical practice since the 1970s of the 20th century (Fagot & David, 1974; Kuhn, 1983). PID refers to an acute, subacute or chronic bacterial infection of the upper female genital tract, that is the cervix (cervicitis), uterus (endometritis), fallopian tubes (salpingitis) and ovaries (oophoritis), which may be sexually transmitted. The insertion, or presence, of an IUD is known to increase the risk of developing PID (Meirik, 2007; Mohllajee, Curtis, & Peterson, 2006; Steen & Shapiro, 2004). The PID-affected patient usually experiences symptoms and signs such as fever, lower abdominal pain, vaginal discharge and irregular bleeding, although PID may be rarely asymptomatic. Common complications are abscesses, infertility, chronic pelvic pain and ectopic pregnancy, but PID may also be complicated by acute septic shock (also called toxic shock syndrome, TSS), which, in turn, can be supported by peritonitis (Jaworski, 1981; Maloy, Meier, & Karl, 1981; Ron-El, Bukovsky, Kharasch, Letko, & Caspi, 1985; Tymon-Rosario, Atrio, Yoon, Erlichman, & Lerner, 2019). The diagnosis of PID relies on clinical signs and symptoms, laboratory testing, histopathology, imaging such as ultrasonography and, very rarely, an explorative laparoscopy or laparotomy may be necessary. Postmortem diagnosis can be confirmed by autopsy. The occurrence of TSS, related to an IUD is very rare (Cho & Fernando, 2013; Klug, Keay, & Ginde, 2009; Romosan, Blidisel, Grigoras, Houtsios, & Ionac, 2013; Venkataramanasetty, Aburawi, & Phillip, 2009). Treatment is based on the administration of antibiotics and support therapy (Brunham, Gottlieb, & Paavonen, 2015; Vanthuyne & Pittrof, 2016).

This case left me with numerous questions, both clinical and scientific, but also with a profound sadness. I reflected on the feeling that most people carry an inner loneliness, which is expressed by incomprehensible behaviours. The deceased woman lived by herself in an isolated rural dwelling but didn't seem in isolation, I never knew if she had a job, but the police report was clear in stating that she had a partner and that, the night before she died, she had dined out in the company of some friends. How long had she had the IUD implanted? How long had she been suffering of pelvic inflammation, before dying of it? Was the development of the septic shock so sudden and intense that she was not able to rely on her cell phone to call for help? It is reported in casework that a few days or weeks may go by with mild and/or aspecific symptoms, such as nausea and lower abdominal pain, but septic shock and death, by multiorgan failure and cardiopulmonary arrest, can develop in a few hours. In this case, the nearest public health centre was just a few kilometres away from the deceased's house, so was the practice of the general practitioner whom she had already referred to in the past, at the time of the spine surgery. Had she ever undergone regular gynaecological checks, as it is routinely recommended after IUD implants? And in the end, is it possible that in an industrialized country in the third millennium a woman can die for a pelvic infection, at night, in an old rural house engulfed by fog, alone like a modern hermit?

Another sombre story relates to a middle-aged woman who, at the time of her death, could have rightfully been called a street character. Mentally disabled since birth, she had always lived with her mother, alternatively on the streets, in institutions and in homeless shelters. The occasional passer-by could observe the inseparable mother and daughter in some of their favourite spots around town, eating and sleeping on steps and benches, or incessantly fussing around considerable piles of tightly packed plastic bags, probably containing all their belongings. I have a personal memory of them enjoying a late summer midday sun on a sidewalk close to the railway station, most likely I was headed to the main hospital and, caught in the excitement of my profession, I simply hurried past them without fostering more thought. I later learnt that the social services kept them constantly monitored, and when they were able to obtain their cooperation, they managed to provide food and medications, but most of all a shelter in the long, dark and chilly winters.

On June 6, 2012, the 44 years old daughter was admitted to the Emergency Room of the city main hospital after being referred by a general practitioner, because of a fall in the institution where she was living. Based on the hospital clinical records, she appeared confused and depressed, could not explain anything about her recent medical history, her body showed numerous bruises in different stages of development, and she could not stand. After setting up a pharmacological treatment based on antibiotics, antiinflammatory and psychoactive drugs, as well as nutritional and electrolytes support, the physicians immediately applied relevant protocols to obtain a diagnosis. The presence of fever, lethargy and low blood pressure with negative imaging and progressive respiratory failure required the transfer of the patient to an Intensive Care Unit (ICU), on suspicion of septic shock, of which she actually died eleven days later.

Following her death, the local health authority requested a clinical autopsy to clarify the nature of the fatal disease, although this procedure is debatable because, if the cause of death is unknown to physicians, the death should be reported for medicolegal investigation. The clinical pathologist suspected an encephalitis, but the only relevant alterations mentioned in the short autopsy report were massive pulmonary oedema and coalescing white areas at the lung sections. After removing the whole brain and collecting samples of every other organ, the clinical pathologist interrupted the autopsy because the case was deemed to require a medicolegal assessment.

I was assigned the case on July 10, 2012, 23 days after the patient's death. Beyond the usual questions about cause, mode and manner of death, the prosecutor inquired about the possibility of medical malpractice on the part of the hospital's treating staff. After a meticulous analysis of the hospital records (which were to all intents and purposes, spotless), I proceeded with an external examination, which turned out to be unremarkable. I then excluded toxicology on the basis that the patient had been hospitalized for eleven days before dying, and any illegal drugs possibly present in her system had been either washed out by, or heavily mixed with, the medication given in the course of her hospital stay. The only hope to get any answer about the cause of death, beyond being natural, relied on histopathology. The starting point was the confirmation, or the exclusion, of the suspected encephalitis. I sent some brain samples embedded in paraffin wax to an esteemed neuropathology expert, who observed *"sparse small lacunar lesions located in the subcortical cerebral white matter and to a lesser extent in the basal nuclei... Numerous extraparenchymal as well as penetrating blood vessels show thickening of the wall, proliferation of the tunica media and... of the intima... some degree of subpial and subependymal gliosis... the hilus of the nucleus dentatus shows, beside vascular changes and perivascular gliosis, myelin loss... the dentate neurons have hypoxia-related changes, with shrunken nuclei and hypereosinophilic cytoplasm. In the tegmentum of the caudal portion of medulla oblongata... there are fairly symmetric lesions, characterized by tissue loss, astrogliosis, petechial hemorrages... focal extravasation of erythrocytes is visible also in the midbrain..."* but *"no obvious signs of cerebral infection"* (Reproduced with permission by Dr. F. R. W. Van de Goot—Department of Pathology, VU University Medical Centre, Amsterdam, The Netherlands). In the meantime, I went on analysing samples from the other organs and tissues collected at the autopsy. The heart showed mild myocardial and coronary arteries sclerosis, the liver presented massive steatosis with widespread foci of cirrhosis/hepatocellular carcinoma, kidneys, adrenal glands, spleen, other abdominal and the pelvic organs did not show any major alterations, and finally the lungs revealed the source of the infection which led to the fatal septic shock: a fungal bronchopneumonia, with fungal hyphae and spores within some bronchi, as well as numerous foci with peribronchial granulocyte infiltration in the lung parenchyma.

Fungal pneumonia is a rare condition, which usually affects immunocompromised individuals and/or hospitalized patients (Goldman, Johnson, & Sarosi, 1999). It can be severe and progress to death because it is untreated by the broad-spectrum antibiotics commonly used for community-acquired and hospital-acquired pneumonia (Davies, 1994; Dermawan, Ghosh, Keating, Gopalakrishna, & Mukhopadhyay, 2018). The most commonly involved microrganisms are *Candida* spp. (albicans, glabrata, tropicalis etc.) and *Aspergillus* spp. (flavus, fumigatus, niger, etc.) (Barkauskas, 2009).

Candida spp. are part of the normal flora of skin and mucosal membranes of the oral cavity and gastrointestinal tract. *Candida* pneumonia occurs primarily as a result of contamination of the lungs following hematogenous dissemination, or it may follow the aspiration of colonized oropharyngeal or gastric contents. At present, the only method to identify *Candida* as the primary lung pathogen is to demonstrate the presence of yeast cells or pseudohyphae in a lung biopsy or, occasionally, at autopsy (Kontoyiannis et al., 2002), but lung biopsy is not used in clinical practice for management of patients with suspected *Candida* infection. Histologic criteria for diagnosis of acute pneumonia include the presence of intense neutrophilic infiltration in the interstitium and intra-alveolar spaces of the lung structure, and *Candida* organisms can be histologically identified by morphology. The preferred staining method is Hematoxylin-Eosin and Gomori's methenamine silver. However, *Candida* pneumonia has rarely been reported, and histological confirmation is even more difficult to achieve (Meersseman et al., 2009; Rello, Esandi, Diaz, et al., 1998; Rello, Esandi, Mariscal et al., 1998).

Aspergillus species are ubiquitous environmental moulds that grow on organic matter and aerosolize conidia. The diagnosis of invasive lung aspergillosis, as well as of candidiasis, relies on clinical examination, culture, histopathology, imaging and detection of the fungal components or, in the case of *Aspergillus*, nucleic acid of species by PCR. The treatment of fungal pneumonia is medical and support, and may need to last several months (Barnes & Marr, 2006; Maertens, Meersseman, & Van Bleyenbergh, 2009; Toleuova, Tayzhanova, Toyynbekova, & Beysenbekova, 2018).

The deceased woman was not clinically immunocompromised, like other individuals reported in the literature (Blaschke, Don, Schillinger, & Rüchel, 2002), but her hepatic cirrhosis/carcinoma might have hindered or prevented a competent immune response against an opportunistic fungal infection, such as candidiasis or aspergillosis. The apparent lack of immunodeficiency prevented the hospital physicians to suspect a fungal pneumonia, and this misled them in the search of the possible localization of the infection, which soon evolved to septic shock. Neither were they helped by comprehensive laboratory tests, as well as clinical and imaging assessments, because their results were all and consistently negative for fungal infection. Once the clinical diagnosis of the fatal disease, which led to a natural death, had been determined, the case was closed without any malpractice charge.

This case represents an unsettling situation for the forensic pathologist, who is called to intervene in a complicated setting. The subject was an uncooperative patient who died in less than two weeks after having been admitted to a hospital ward, despite a swift transfer to an ICU. However, the outcome could be said to have suffered because of a lack of any correct clinical diagnosis both in the antemortem and in the postmortem period. A result of these possible complications was that there was the potential for a malpractice suit to be lodged. Furthermore, a precise histopathological identification of the fungal species could not be achieved, as the interval between death and autopsy had been too long and the possibility of contamination could not be excluded. My final reflection was that the poor woman died as unaware of what was happening to her as she had always lived.

References

Barkauskas, C. E. (2009). Candida pneumonia: what we know and what we don't. *Current Fungal Infection Reports*, *3*(1), 21. Available from https://doi.org/10.1007/s12281-009-0004-z.

Barnes, P. D., & Marr, K. A. (2006). Aspergillosis: spectrum of disease, diagnosis, and treatment. *Infectious Disease Clinics of North America*, *20*(3), 545. Retrieved from http://murdoch.summon.serialssolutions.com/2.0.0/link/0/eLvHCXMwtV1bS8MwFA7qQHwR73fpD1ilTZu1EX0Y4nAPe3J7HkmTSGE3Nvf_Pbm1W0HRB19KSNJA8qWn5-R85wShBD9EYUMmRClTVGBGVII5qPwxlEGTyASDXyAnzGdnMDTVOqKgQV39L-ChDqDXgbR_AL8aFCqgDFsAnrAJ4PmrbdDVmcA_yslkvioN-82EVi7XU60lOu-MXmZhKXc244BhVXoG-qb62nfUrfXKv-tCKw0hZMsHVB-RLv1tACBWJ_OFrEnGA7a0lI5SBx26Y9WNIwjqjyCcpKJxSAi2DhbpJCnJQprbAGkval2PctMSN3KT2JySG4AspgaR-uEPzNLc37_zc2kibXTXpFOpTURafz3IWjt53UUtHIxkbo9-rHE6gpxq3tp-JTibrRmgYHEbxGB6hQ2cxBF2L7THakbMTtD9wnIhT9LQF8WPgAQ7mKnAgtYMK3nYA4A-YVuGdo1HsdvryF7k6MULs80zBVWSZEIoVgHZarRKq0IAzU2ELhgmKBOWcFVHMCpjDJZcoVoTJKoJPiNKL4HO3N5jN5iYKMFBgzGRVKxqmKOCedQinQEEUK-oyXZFbqw8x4vbOKTsV-R629bbtBBvUFuUUvBZyTvqru57s2ifwEX7kbo.

Blaschke, S., Don, M., Schillinger, W., & Rüchel, R. (2002). Candida pneumonia in patients without definitive immunodeficiency. *Mycoses*, *45*(Suppl 3), 22. Retrieved from http://murdoch.summon.serialssolutions.com/2.0.0/link/0/eLvHCXMwtV07T8MwELZQERIL4v2uvEepkthxm4GhlFYgYCLMlR07IkPTCrVD_z3nRx5EQoKBJYocKQ9_zum-u_N3CJFoEPgdmwCOLxsBFRMsAf87z3Q7bjgF7wIYCDcqjE2ZatMHsFO6-l_AwxhAArzfS_gH8-qYwAOewBOAIiwCOv1oGE71tRXJvVaoNPLTgXiOmane26cJkqfLCVREREVesPIUg-Yv_5b1vd1q8vbm8A6eN7Zh6vu4aKVoX9wNflNmsckHXQEsS7qM2kenae_n-hq1KZ4sYpBtAOSCSH-kNrOtQNljSg4OX4QuzFnZWnsmT6lHmmby6htxWHmVguDQxgBaU9YRyPbkpbqkpZGX8giW9-p0n9_0_oFMN5Duy_j9HlaZ5KGiWm5V7-nVol1t-gwCeNRpIfowFEBPLagHaEdqY7Rnm0Ouj1BYwcdrqHDRYkr6LCDDjfQ4S50pyidTdP-Jo-8aXvgrIOp-LoG85lo9iXGShRLIomCBHBEZxLEQsVYyMiZzRKWUPBhK-KHA3xSCRQGJM3KGeuWyVBcIqySmLAyVFkuiYchEziNFQ8oVmGCR00t0bj99vrKiJvNqU-q5-vHKN9k0rHBN_ukG99edG3dZtt_rARJ5mfTf9X1DdOaQ.

Brunham, R. C., Gottlieb, S. L., & Paavonen, J. (2015). Pelvic inflammatory disease. *The New England Journal of Medicine*, *372*(21), 2039–2048. Available from https://doi.org/10.1056/NEJMra1411426.

Cho, E. E. M. D., & Fernando, D. M. D. M. P. H. (2013). Fatal streptococcal toxic shock syndrome from an intrauterine device. *Journal of Emergency Medicine*, *44*(4), 777–780. Available from https://doi.org/10.1016/j.jemermed.2012.03.020.

Davies, S. F. (1994). Fungal pneumonia. *Medical Clinics of North America*, *78*(5), 1049–1065. Available from https://doi.org/10.1016/s0025-7125(16)30119-5.

Dermawan, J. K. T., Ghosh, S., Keating, M. K., Gopalakrishna, K. V., & Mukhopadhyay, S. (2018). Candida pneumonia with severe clinical course, recovery with antifungal therapy and unusual pathologic findings: a case report. *Medicine*, *97* (2), e9650. Available from https://doi.org/10.1097/MD.0000000000009650.

Fagot, R., & David, M. P. (1974). A report of four cases with serious complications after insertion of an intrauterine contraceptive device (author's transl). *Geburtshilfe und Frauenheilkunde*, *34*(3), 164. Retrieved from http://murdoch.summon.serialssolutions.com/2.0.0/link/0/eLvHCXMwtV07T8MwELaACtQF8RSvotsAoaAmMXkMDBWiwMBEmSs3cWhEm1Y0sPDnubPdNIkAwcASRXFiOfku57PvuzvGXOeibdV0ghcIEfk-DT3gDV_oDP2yHwndoLnfRnvCK7AyKprpw8Naoq_8FPF5D6CmQ9g_gF53iBTxHEcAjCgEefyUGHeMVIKMwwQfOI5y2TEgbDYAYsFVaua4anmbkpjfWpCA6ZP4q-qPwDWaWK3y4UIeZdxV2htiFTFW8YGhdATnPgaL7PYKzfW4kQ5rNhOkokFeAl-s_lNZkOZjl4omK0QJvE8yStsRkW9V5u3JiAt1pF7Pl8wtebK1_YscvOUla_ZyUzLa3-OlSW2d3LwE0XSsMOKBGwS6MOePjbU02vMWyqg-jtMov5KZ9fS4zBoUnKSWHPfdwv_EQ1U0txhyk62aDmrLD2WG9DbYulk_QEcjvcmWYrnF1h4MQ2KbfXRAA-w6TBAhwUIADAQ4GcKgADgpwKACnB0UGZcChAjhowOFUw30yAw322Q5rdW9613eWHnp_qjOZ9M07ObtsJZtkco8Bd2QQ2pFww4hzETrCjy957ASJ79qU-m2f7X7dx8F3DYesuZCGI9ZI8M-SraJc17H68J-8nVZ5.

Goldman, M., Johnson, P. C., & Sarosi, G. A. (1999). Fungal pneumonias. The endemic mycoses. *Clinics in chest medicine*, *20*(3), 507. Retrieved from http://murdoch.summon.serialssolutions.com/2.0.0/link/0/eLvHCXMwtV07T8MwELaASogF8X6jTGypEid-ZGBAiBYGJspcXWJbQqJppdKBf8_5kTRqhYCBJYpsyZHvO1_uzvcgJKP9JP6RCSC04RJQOy9NwguWqcr2FqGVyhVIVTXVGVyYatPSfS109b-AxzGE3ibS_gH8dlEcwHdkAXwiE-DzV2wwwMNsk61qvcBvvsG874IsrOPbRsVPPm3A-ryrovpKoS5M1jXTWrt-H07fVfCbtm6b0GjL6aQdxyvgP9iFCwyDz1SFhLtlAFUjhqhw5qof0kFMMvy3UZ8l2chRmnT4JesIReb72naoPZs4cqNuZ2_pkp9nV2pit1O2PvoEifBxq-v49WWT9GyqkTMgngbtbRIqRS5tvtmJrRQbVlixJpxWMdoju8EciO48cPtkQ9cHZPs5UPyQ3-Hj8og5-EeIXBfyigN8RGQ0eRvePcWhtEc_QJI9LQRloxWQhAVADTIVQKpMCclZoaQv0lJwDEpjxLC2BViCrxBgtFGXSeu2OyVY9rfUpiURaVJxqkeXGFlpKi9JInQK-nBaR42tQZOfEbHM98-ZJxs_Xzb2cuyM6SEy5Jz-Bh0Fdth61rR90v-Pwttg.

Jaworski, E. (1981). Case of tubo-ovarian abscesses with peritonitis and septic shock in a patient wearing an intrauterine contraceptive device. *Wiadomosci lekarskie (Warsaw, Poland: 1960)*, *34*(5), 431. Retrieved from http://murdoch.summon.serialssolutions.com/2.0.0/link/0/eLvHCXMwtV1LSwMxEA5qEXoRRYuvytzLynbfPXiQ0qKeBCs9lmQfuPSxxdYK_npnkuw2Fot68LIsmyVs8yXTmck3XxhznWvb2rAJQjiCcztxgj-gKIzuNQzcOItHxI5H5flqpM0ia6lbq6n8Bj88Qeiqk_QP4Vaf4AO9xCuAVJwFefzUN-ulwl65dvorCKFUbGuKA5GgvSDNelbSR2vKS1nSvB5gUxXeLW4gVtJeVDeKm-2nrH4VFVjaQz8crpPAhyUyXhnUuGzEoWYmlGXen2DnOeFFPSzWxN0jHG0uNc-rZDvOVyc-mxIIqlTlAEtpGgeCBVV326dm-dpGh3IoOlVRpez7XQNwtNw6uzmLm5tS2tqKf-GAx45lOJT-jQNmf0Y-OGhHbZQmrq0ySPlzfpzHp-2mU1KkyS4cZ9v8rMoVOGcXKnpCbQV9fZvu5jI_qQXsjgkB3o8AFuFdBHbGc-OWYfBDIUGZggQwUyEMhggAw40qBABgky5Pg6aJBBg4xvgQkyfAEZFMgnrNnvDbp3lvrc0VyJl4z073AabG9WzNJTBkGMPm3QSTLuC89zs8hNwnbGwzBIHeHG8RlrfN_H-baGC1ZfT4JLVstwMaXN6oSuKznen2i9Urc.

Klug, C. D. M. D., Keay, C. R. M. D., & Ginde, A. A. M. D. M. P. H. (2009). Fatal toxic shock syndrome from an intrauterine device. *Annals of Emergency Medicine*, *54* (5), 701–703. Available from https://doi.org/10.1016/j.annemergmed.2009.05.030.

Kontoyiannis, D. P., Reddy, B. T., Torres, H. A., Luna, M., Lewis, R. E., Tarrand, J., … Raad, I. I. (2002). Pulmonary candidiasis in patients with cancer: an autopsy study. *Clinical Infectious Diseases*, *34*(3), 400–403. Available from https://doi.org/10.1086/338404.

Kuhn, W. (1983). Emergency in general medicine (43). Septic complications in implanted IUD. *Zeitschrift fur Allgemeinmedizin*, *59*(2), 79. Retrieved from http://murdoch.summon.serialssolutions.com/2.0.0/link/0/eLvHCXMwtV07T8MwED4BFVIXBIKKV5FHUJSocUybDgwRtKIz7dKlKo0tLLWhqtqFX8-dnbghPAQDGazEjhzrvtPlzr4HQMSDll-RCcoE94jWjIvbUIWyI-VMTY0yjQp42imyMxg31W2BwYrr6n8Bj30IPQXS_gF8Nyl24D2yALbIBNj-ig16LrxSZ1Qumbag3IE6qZeCtloDlBlLSt36ycNc4zMRP_UGo4eyJjvuJ4E3lnqN5vFKq7WnNisvmc_Jl4ZcDFL9prcn_JuXzHnz2U2GsBuTi5XPWyW5KKLIR6TCsuDMU3nrkv1qpaAtD1Oi7nJhyNuOeZdbr-kfBysZsIsRSoa-QPqs72Tmj552oUZxRcZaGPSL3y-ymcm96lZch_18gorlYDSI4SEc5Ko_SyxIR7CTymMYOICYzlgOECsAYtciugmYBYd9AIded-AwBOcEmv3e8P7Rt1-fLG0ekUm-LN6Avew1k6fA0ljyWCpJl-BiNp0-x7LdjlGNFzgWnkHj6znOvxu4gPoWz0uoKeRr2XTFsq4M7d4BpTQk-g.

Maertens, J., Meersseman, W., & Van Bleyenbergh, P. (2009). New therapies for fungal pneumonia. *Current Opinion in Infectious Diseases*, *22*(2), 183–190. Available from https://doi.org/10.1097/QCO.0b013e328328cfff.

Maloy, A. L., Meier, F. A., & Karl, R. C. (1981). Fatal peritonitis following IUD-associated salpingitis. *Obstetrics and gynecology*, *58*(3), 397. Retrieved from http://murdoch.summon.serialssolutions.com/2.0.0/link/0/eLvHCXMwtV3dS8MwEA_ToexF_Bp-03fpaJu0TR8Eh1oUGYJuzyNpEhlsXXED8b_3knRdN1T0wZcQEggkv8vl7rj8DiEc-dDx3TScISngUECxBwhjliZSRCDJ4ijFPCPP4gp3BpKk2Gtdfp67-F_AwBtDrj7R_AL9aFAagDyIALQgBtL8Sg9RUB9F0xnN9e0eafmE8nr6bRIHBrctKeMDunLFxYcoXj-WZ1k_WJgyBoHn_L5vz6kctsJRbfY2Mb0OteVpHknhxZWUiXwdJH9mbizc9lZFbY-z3fUr5Kplrn_iRtTy9jYkVZl0hi7ATZVfSudGtKa7OCagsQ2G7d28sXEHH0MlkJiSw-v8OLnGjr2Y0UTpEzHK5lcydwcvG6ip_xwZT-IhrZ5mzTyzyPnR22ihrXKBNa_CWBf9XbRTugVO1wK4hxoy30fbvTLx4QBFBkenhqNT4eis4ujUcDxE_fSuf3PvliUv3CLx-qCvijIcC9KJUGWdE0IwkNADNKATzeeJTpcCjjISCLvZxBP5oLMHiJIozgRUJ2m-gzn-byCDkxDUOcxZ6ScPdIlDCmCA9iBhcw5F4WHqO23fCwsLQmw_IkTr6bOEWtpUycoaaCKyLPq7pbF-aoPwG0pjkx.

Meersseman, W., Lagrou, K., Spriet, I., Maertens, J., Verbeken, E., Peetermans, W. E., & Van Wijngaerden, E. (2009). Significance of the isolation of Candida species from airway samples in critically ill patients: a prospective, autopsy study. *Intensive care medicine*, *35*(9), 1526–1531. Available from https://doi.org/10.1007/s00134-009-1482-8.

Meirik, O. (2007). Intrauterine devices — upper and lower genital tract infections. *Contraception*, *75*(6), S41–S47. Available from https://doi.org/10.1016/j.contraception.2006.12.017.

Mohllajee, A. P., Curtis, K. M., & Peterson, H. B. (2006). Does insertion and use of an intrauterine device increase the risk of pelvic inflammatory disease among women with sexually transmitted infection? A systematic review. *Contraception*, *73*(2), 145–153. Available from https://doi.org/10.1016/j.contraception.2005.08.007.

Rello, J., Esandi, M.-E., Diaz, E., Mariscal, D., Gallego, M., & Vallès, J. (1998). The role of Candida sp isolated from bronchoscopic samples in nonneutropenic patients. *Chest*, *114*(1), 146–149. Available from https://doi.org/10.1378/chest.114.1.146.

Rello, J., Esandi, M.-E., Mariscal, D., Gallego, M., Domingo, C., & Valles, J. (1998). Invasive pulmonary Aspergillosis in patients with chronic obstructive pulmonary disease: report of eight cases and review. *Clinical Infectious Diseases*, *26*(6), 1473–1475. Available from https://doi.org/10.1086/517672.

Romosan, G., Blidisel, A., Grigoras, D., Houtsios, A., & Ionac, M. (2013). Meningococcal septic shock after IUD insertion, a case presentation. *Revista medico-chirurgicala a Societatii de Medici si Naturalisti din Iasi*, *117*(4), 929. Retrieved from http://murdoch.summon.serialssolutions.com/2.0.0/link/0/eLvHCXMwtV1Lb4JAEN7YeumladP3K3unNLAsIocejG3VQ0_Vs2GXpZIoGNH_33ldBDRp0x56IYYNGnY-Z-fxzQwhHnty7D2dIFTIfTgpPBE7CkxuX7hwUDq-8rD7C6-6M2iaaqu15b7vUVf_S_BwD0SPhbR_EH71pXADPgME4AoggOuvYPCuMPCRg9rT5Y_IYZFWMQMtWI4HH01ekJCO9GqTgI8sCScbNg_Y1iVlTQsWkwlgUZqkfG7LWbrarLT6jOBRQwKFh1IrViYLlFpFipxo7O-BCsWC09IaRUVa53oWeWHisINymLcOEMxTzB7NdwKug1X6CaAtdrjKw3yzLlLDF-w1wxhuTYirVDPv2kHXtN2sVLOp6ywxyBuKNjRxkoYElwstQsZ9sIDNWJefV_f6bFdL2HN9AduzflaZPfk4IG0sX9JOyeit1lV-sNNXB_Qga2RoWQiOYrfOKIOd4GNvPEN4MG-KjajLH91zarRxMz4hx6VXQnsGP6ekpbIz0t_BDjXYoRo7VGOHAnZohZ1HGlFEDm0i55yM317H_aFdztywlzzw7KQbRNJToWRuJxJOR6jY9aWDVHUGJyGPJQvAx_VCIcDPZXHCFPeEjKUX-4GrGLsgh1meqStCHSFgf3DEXQesRBGEEdimIZdBkrhJx4mvyaV55enS9FWZbjfj5tuVW3JUY-eOtBP4l6r7avTXgxbRFwnOYO0.

Ron-El, R., Bukovsky, I., Kharasch, J., Letko, Y., & Caspi, E. (1985). Pneumococcal peritonitis with the presence of an intrauterine device. *International Journal of Gynaecology and Obstetrics*, *23*(4), 339. Retrieved from http://murdoch.summon.serialssolutions.com/2.0.0/link/0/eLvHCXMwtV1LS8QwEA6rongRn_gmf6DSpt0-Dh5EXRUVBd3zkldFdNvFrYL_3pkmfWxB1IOXsjTLQDNfJ5P0m28I8dmR63RiApMpLES-e7CfK14n2XSElQMdH6RbFSzXjhqba61Xl-B3q6n85Hu6B67GQ9g_Or43CDfgNEIArgACuv4LBfabfxzlEPfQFqhoX-BI_26I2UyeFBUiyPDvgyHss3jj2ecD0U-kPy42rEtjZE8SW7sTTZ8a1bBSdcgH4Qfn_aUUdqdUqyk5SFTlh1uAAtS3qLPaiY_Outtl8J8qc89d-Z4uP7S_7RPRK-Rl3qqWl7VZ-M3-jiJW_WIGWKAeN-Te5qahFcbMZr4rk2ITyOEgfrY9sx3tQ0WywHrYDtGymlFhIm4xIKLA5RmebHwY5adzWCwu1j9SyLY505w4c5s-oA1UOXO5mpQpwpe5JmWjvYxlsmiNdDZ5ZTZzuMqWbHbFHpiALVGejpbJ0u3l-oixQc7auKItXFHEFQXH0gpXNE8pz2gbV9TgapMMB-ePp5eObcjhSAYT6oTYpCWARUBLT-nYVZC9CxVFmgvYJQgh_SRM3FQHSPAVnDNcMFBgkCkRJEKwLTKf5ZneJjTiMmTwryAW_SANXRFgH4Eg5srljPflDtkyzz-aGNWVkZ2Y3e8G9shyA5F9spDCG6wP6rZgh-XMfwEvdXPg.

Steen, R., & Shapiro, K. (2004). Intrauterine contraceptive devices and risk of pelvic inflammatory disease: standard of care in high STI prevalence settings. *Reproductive Health Matters*, *12*(23), 136–143. Available from https://doi.org/10.1016/S0968-8080(04)23123-8.

Toleuova, A., Tayzhanova, D., Toyynbekova, R., & Beysenbekova, Z. (2018). Case report of Candida pneumonia. *Georgian medical news(Issue)*, *86*. Retrieved from http://murdoch.summon.serialssolutions.com/2.0.0/link/0/eLvHCXMwtV1LT4NAEN6ovXgxGt-PZu9NTZdX4eCBAI1c2qalFy8NLGuaKNA01qT-emd3eaw1NXrwQsgMGch8wzA7zM4gpGv3ve6WT3BSynpOSlhqWjGDb55NYqprJjUg3KYxqboziDLVat74t9LV_wIeaAA930j7B_BroUCAczABOIIRwPFXZuC506AzCcajScQLfDx36Ie-2xkPgxloLnTV4FTkx_kLn5V_b9SQOype2bp4j7_kP2G9_7GI85LsN9duNnnCXkp6U5MIZs-MUxtNCTToQu6pTbvykqOggmmIiYlyg4gtli2tFx8tMKFlzwEsY0vf_zN3qhF2zeFf0-DBTx9sDy7my6j1p8g5FYNoSDOsMGwSiYmSgrqJ6Wt34uhWwtI0Q4ER2jo3IdgF2-J2AnaW61PEeZoYYkWHg1wiRau0TpD7UEQeY9dKXS-lL1C5tXttHN0kBc5u0TYsVKdmoTyIfSGoetJYvaZrdHEsUjS7yVX6GKHkOudnBt02MB0i1rPYL7srp6J1Raa-QSlXBTH.

Tymon-Rosario, J., Atrio, J. M., Yoon, H. A., Erlichman, D., & Lerner, V. (2019). Streptococcus constellatus peritonitis and subsequent septic shock following intrauterine device removal. *Case Reports in Obstetrics and Gynecology*, *2019*, 6491617-6491615. Available from https://doi.org/10.1155/2019/6491617.

Vanthuyne, A., & Pittrof, R. (2016). Diagnosis and treatment of pelvic inflammatory disease. *Prescriber*, *27*(10), 47–50. Available from https://doi.org/10.1002/psb.1507.

Venkataramanasetty, R., Aburawi, A., & Phillip, H. (2009). Streptococcal toxic shock syndrome following insertion of an intrauterine device - A case report. *The European Journal of Contraception and Reproductive Health Care*, *14*(5), 379–382. Available from https://doi.org/10.3109/13625180903149159.

CHAPTER 2

Fatal insulin overdose: a case and a short overview

Edda Emanuela Guareschi[1] and Paola Annarosa Magni[1,2]
[1]Medical, Molecular and Forensic Sciences, College of Science, Health, Engineering and Education, Murdoch University, Murdoch, WA, Australia, [2]Murdoch University Singapore, Singapore

ABSTRACT
A case of suicide by insulin overdose is apparently simple to handle and file, but it triggers more than a few questions and reflections, both because it is rare and because the postmortem assessment can be quite complex. In this example the deceased person was not immediately identified, and the body was found in the open and close to a water source (creek). Critical information, such as clinical and psychiatric history, and/or a farewell letter, were missing, the body had been hastily moved from the death scene by rescue staff. An entomology expert was also needed for the estimation of the postmortem interval (PMI). The external examination and the autopsy ruled out external violence, but the decomposition stage prevented any reliable identification of injection marks. Postmortem biochemistry on blood was consistent with the hypothesis of hypoglycemic encephalopathy by insulin overdose with suicidal intent as cause, mode and manner of death. A short review of up to date literature on insulin overdoses is also outlined, with the aim of providing solid scientific references for similar cases.

Keywords: Insulin; overdose; postmortem biochemistry; suicide; hypoglycemic encephalopathy; identification; forensic entomology

When a pathologist's career approaches a decade, one might feel confident enough to suppose that the reason why a case seems ordinary is because it actually is. However, cases initially deemed ordinary can nevertheless be stimulating, and arouse the curiosity to broaden one's knowledge about specific subjects.

Forensic Pathology Case Studies. DOI: https://doi.org/10.1016/B978-0-12-824294-0.00004-2

Figure 2.1 Death scene investigation.

In late April 2011, a body had been found under a small country bridge in the outskirts of town, and I was requested to check the recovery scene (Fig. 2.1).

When I arrived at the scene the body had already been removed, a perfunctory practice happening all too often, and for which everybody involved always offers a convincing explanation, so I just acknowledged the isolated location of a country creek, with its small bridge and surrounding wide crop fields punctuated by intricated lush green woods. The police report filled me in with the details of an apparently middle-aged male, fully clothed, found dead and supine on the edge of the creek water, with a small leather bag containing several vials containing insulin, syringes for insulin injection and two empty insulin pens (Lantus and Humalog) in the internal fold of his jacket. The body's face was, according to the report, "almost completely covered by maggots".

Beyond cause, mode and manner of death, the prosecutor considered critical to know the time of death, or postmortem interval (PMI). In fact, since the deceased had not yet been identified, the assessment of PMI was necessary to exclude any potential identities. The body showed a massive presence of insect larvae, especially around the face orifices (mouth, nose, eyes and ears) (Fig. 2.2).

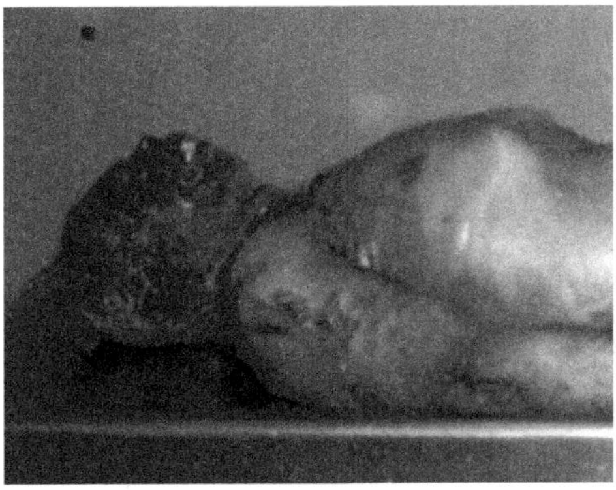

Figure 2.2 Colonization of the body's face by insect larvae.

When bodies are highly decomposed and colonized by insects the use of the insect in aiding in the estimation of the time since death (medico-legal entomology or forensic entomology) is recommended (Byrd & Castner, 2010). Insects—especially carrion flies and beetles—are attracted by the odours of the decomposition and can colonize the body shortly after death. Depending upon the species and the environmental factors—mainly temperature—it is possible to use growth tables to age the insects and thereby provide an estimation of the time since death based on the time of insect colonization.

Accordingly with the best practice and guidelines for forensic entomology (Amendt et al., 2007), insect larvae were carefully collected from the different areas of colonization using a plastic spoon, placed in containers and labelled accordingly. The use of the spoon facilitated the random collection of a large number of larvae, representative of the different species present and the different stages in life cycles. Two subsamples were collected, one for immediate preservation and one for species confirmation. For the immediate preservation, larvae were killed using hot water and preserved in 70% ethanol. For the species confirmation, the specimens where placed in a ventilated container in a fridge at 2°C–4°C. This was repeated for samples taken at the death scene and during autopsy. Furthermore, a temperature data-logger was placed at the death scene and left for ten days, in order to obtain information regarding the environmental temperature of the death scene which could be compared with equivalent data from the closest meteorological station. A correct temperature data-set of the period prior to the body discovery is pivotal to ensure the best possible accuracy of the PMI estimation using the entomological method.

All the samples, the images of the crime scene and autopsy, as well as the temperature data and the thermal history of the samples, were provided to a specialist in forensic entomology two days after the autopsy. Samples stored in ethanol were used to identify the insect species and their life stage, while samples stored in the fridge were used for species identification purposes as it is often necessary to allow the various insect larvae to grow to maturity to be certain of correct species identification (Smith, 1986). The entomologist reported the presence of larvae of *Calliphora vomitoria (L.)* (Diptera: Calliphoridae) in the third instar of their life cycle, a common species found especially in the rural areas of the Holoartic region during winter and spring (Smith, 1986). Considering the environmental data and the presence of a larval mass, the colonization was aged as 4–5 days old. As the body was completely exposed to the insect colonization and the weather didn't register any cold peaks or high levels of rainfall, it is reasonable to assume that the time since death was close to this timeline. However, it is important to underline that the effects of insulin on the insect colonization and growth rate has yet to be investigated in entomotoxicology (Chophi, Sharma, Sharma, & Singh, 2019).

The external examination revealed an initial chromatic stage of putrefaction—more advanced on the face—which, given the environmental circumstances, could definitely rule out a longer PMI. No apparent traumatic injuries were noticed at the external examination, but unfortunately the shades and the diversified patches of the skin colour proved too challenging to discern any injection marks, which I supposed had to be there in order to confirm the suspicion of a fatal insulin overdose. Insulin injection is subcutaneous and requires the use of short (5–6 mm),

Table 2.1 Postmortem biochemistry on blood.

Blood chemiluminescence test	Concentration	Reference range
Insulin	3.0 μU/ml	2.0–25.0
C-peptide	0.01 ng/ml	0.80–4.00

fine needles. As a consequence, the resulting injection marks are tinier than ordinary intra-venous injection marks. The internal examination was negative for traumas and presented aspecific signs of asphyxia, such as pulmonary oedema and diffuse subpleural petechial haemorrhage. Toxicology results on blood and urine matrixes were inconspicuous, but postmortem biochemistry on blood was consistent with insulin overdose as reported in the scientific literature (Table 2.1).

The hypothesis of insulin overdose was also consistent with both the (scarce) information on the circumstances of death and the amount of insulin once held in the two recovered empty pens (total dose of 600 International Units-IU). Therapeutic doses of insulin vary between 0.2 and 1.1 IU/kg of body weight/day, and are divided in three or four daily administrations. The average build of the deceased suggested a maximum daily dose of 90 IU. The total insulin dose held in the numerous vials and two pens amounted to a 1000 IU, and it would have certainly led to hypoglycemic coma. The insulin content of the two pens alone, 600 IU, would also have achieved the purpose. Accordingly, the case was closed as a suicide by insulin overdose, which through hypoglycemic coma causes a condition of encephalopathy leading to irreversible damage to the Central Nervous System (Auer, 2004). The deceased was identified by cross-comparison of data on missing persons. Through the physical description, the tattoos and an estimated PMI of 4–5 days, the police were able to identify the body as belonging to a 48 years old European Union citizen who resided 400 km southeast of the place where his body was recovered.

In forensic pathology, insulin overdoses are classified as either accidental (Batalis & Prahlow, 2004; Kuhn & Cantrell, 2008) or intentional. Insulin is a physiological hormone which regulates glucose metabolism, its deficiency or a resistance offered by biological tissues characterizes diabetes mellitus. Several types of insulins, differing in the rapidity of acting from ultra-rapid to long-acting, are commercialized as medications in substitutive treatments. Insulin-based drugs hold a narrow therapeutic index, that is the difference between therapeutic and toxic doses is small. Insulin administration is subcutaneous and directly self-administered by most diabetic patients. Intentional insulin overdoses can be administered with homicidal intents, an event rarely reported in the literature (Marks, 2009; Marks & Richmond, 2008; Tong et al., 2017), or as a means of suicide (Beastall, Gibson, & Martin, 1995; Hänsch & De Roy, 1977; Nikolic, Atanasijevic, & Popovic, 2006). While prompt treatment holds a favourable prognosis, especially in the case of unintentional and low-dose insulin overdoses—which can sometimes be treated at home (Beuhler, Spiller, & Aleguas, 2013; Glogan, Levitan, Brooks, & Gerkin, 2013)—delayed or absent treatment leads to progressive hypoglycaemia, hypoglicemic coma and death (Russell, Stevens, & Stern, 2009).

Different studies report doses and biochemistry profiles of insulin intentional overdoses, with total administered insulin doses ranging from 100 to 4800 IU (Johansen & Christensen, 2018; Kernbach-Wighton & Püschel, 1998). Treatment options include intra venous glucose administration, whereas glucagon, octreotide, hydrocortisone treatment and oral intake of complex carbohydrates, or surgical incision are proposed alternatives (McIntyre, Woolf, & Burnham, 1986). Postmortem detection of insulin overdoses can be an elaborate procedure, ranging from the possible discovery of injection marks at the external examination, to histopathology and immunohistochemistry on organs samples like brain, heart, liver, kidney and skin, to postmortem biochemistry. Immunohistochemistry methods can be used to detect insulin in subcutaneous soft tissues at the injection sites (Lutz, Pedal, Wetzel, & Mattern, 1997). Histological findings list neuronal degeneration and astrocyte proliferation in the central nervous system, epithelial necrosis in both the proximal and distal renal tubules, and minor or aspecific changes in heart and liver (Tong et al., 2017). Postmortem biochemical screening is usually considered to be the gold standard in overdose cases. However, postmortem analysis of insulin and C-peptide -a peptide released during cleavage of insulin from proinsulin pro-hormone-does not deliver any reliable insulin dosage estimation because of the rapid occurrence of decomposition changes and blood haemolysis after death (Palmiere et al., 2015). The estimated lower limit for a lethal dosage is 100 I.U. (range 100–3000 IU) (Kernbach-Wighton & Püschel, 1998). Furthermore, the assessment of the postmortem molar ratio of insulin to C peptide—$0.12 \pm 0.47–1.0$ in a healthy living individual—is suggested as positive evidence for insulin overdose, because it reveals injection of exogenous insulin in life (Iwase, Kobayashi, Nakajima, & Takatori, 2001). Finally, postmortem serum insulin concentrations have tentatively been related to the duration of ante mortem hypoglycaemia (Shibutani & Ogawa, 2000).

This case started quite simply, with a middle-aged man who travelled a long distance to find a quiet place to end his life. He probably succeeded in the achievement of a peaceful final act, but the process of the determination of the cause of death by insulin overdose on an unidentified and partially decomposed body may prove far from peaceful and fluid, because critical information, such as clinical and psychiatric history, and/or a farewell letter were missing, and the decomposition process heavily interferes with pathomorphological findings, postmortem biochemistry and toxicology.

References

Amendt, J., Campobasso, C. P., Gaudry, E., Reiter, C., LeBlanc, H. N., Hall, M. J. R., … European Association for Forensic Entomology. (2007). Best practice in forensic entomology—standards and guidelines. *International Journal of Legal Medicine*, *121*(2), 90–104. Available from https://doi.org/10.1007/s00414-006-0086-x.

Auer, R. N. (2004). Hypoglycemic brain damage. *Metabolic Brain Disease*, *19*(3), 169–175. Available from https://doi.org/10.1023/B:MEBR.0000043967.78763.5b.

Batalis, N. I., & Prahlow, J. A. (2004). Accidental insulin overdose. *Journal of Forensic Sciences*, *49*(5), 1117. Retrieved from http://murdoch.summon.serialssolutions.com/2.0.0/

link/0/eLvHCXMwtV1LS8QwEA7qXgQR349V6V26NGmTNgcPi7joTdj1vKSZFES3u6D_HyePPlwR9eAllAYC88jkm8lkhpCUjZJ4zSZoJqRSIDgUBXAFTAMrlDGclYhpu-oMLk21aS3_JXX1vwSP_1D09iHtH4TfLoo_8BtVAEdUAhx_pQZjrW3b0HdXW8OnndukT-Vi-fc4B6nApolib1K6vw-HYxdGVq5YY9Oeli7c-osF69XdE_kIhBEibYELWZkv1k_sp9Y2hRybYRC6smyn7RtPXGQ3KwXsWEG1n3jfNyI7VwjEXwZpAdEd_nl2rgN1O2WroC3jW7zemjp-mm2RgHxY5d-Fh0p6_ggra1Ii3pLjOS36FNd_BYYjZHtkNTI7GXkz7ZMPUB2THR04j_yDskAw7kUVBZFEjsiMyndzNbu_j0MIiXqHfFlOTFkqaEpRKUs3SlIMGjRApySHHPcAroaREIhIGiMUzQPTGjK40ur1GMnZMtuplbU5JlGSGSsgEqBQy3D4FVzkvOZNViQeUyc7IiadsvvJVSuYNzeffzgzJdqcDF2RQoc6by7aR1pVj6we9kCd6.

Beastall, G. H., Gibson, I. H., & Martin, J. (1995). Successful suicide by insulin injection in a non-diabetic. *Medicine, Science, and the Law*, *35*(1), 79. Retrieved from http://murdoch.summon.serialssolutions.com/2.0.0/link/0/eLvHCXMwtV07T8MwELbaTiyIV0V5VJ66oFR5OI0zMLSI0iIhhpY5chwbBYmASjvw7znbcR6dYGCJIkt5-buc78533yEU-GPX2dMJhIUedcGSIyKdkDglhFMuiUdFJgOimZXqNNVOx7JC7KWu_hfwMAbQq0LaP4Bf3RQG4BxEAI4gBHD8lRisdrojospE_trlPM-EMjhtBnpevAlu0x3ZTfFROCYYm_Om1fpUbsDrUKlRBjbrU9mtjUD4TLUCYmYr42FcbUPVbcqX9W-DNYPBYxx5MLXcr9qDYl1XYshky05FiG8WwBQMhLISmVNoqXcNR0hIuo0FN-a5k2MfZstSgd3zY19tTT-0YTb6R40t9hKra3onBeVl3UBd2lYjeLZ7suhyQKqW3gq16nWoRb_oS2K9ZH6LB0CPDUQHeMOqI4QV2Y0lMU1-DhEjycfuMSPFyBB2eY4SZ4Z2g9v1_fLZyy1YXzSmHFCXjss1SxTJGUMAZ_S8wiT1ApucvACOOCSF-EYDuGrsfg0yZCRsRnUezBr-TKoI968BRxjnCQRb7ens1S1YqMKn9xEkomUhJngrABGqmvTpQIbzeMs7IMA65WTGBJNacD1Dfzknwa3pMEdHtEqHvx2ztcooNaaK5Qb7v-ZieuqT9cQXJflfKgx-gEAX0wH.

Beuhler, M. C., Spiller, H. A., & Aleguas, A. (2013). Demographics and outcome of unintentional insulin overdoses managed by three poison centers. *Clinical Toxicology*, *51*(8), 789–793. Available from https://doi.org/10.3109/15563650.2013.829236.

Byrd, J. H., & Castner, J. L. (2010). *Forensic entomology – The utility of arthropods in legal investigation* (2nd ed.). Boca Raton, FL, USA: CRC Press.

Chophi, R., Sharma, S., Sharma, S., & Singh, R. (2019). Forensic entomotoxicology: Current concepts, trends and challenges. *Journal of Forensic and Legal Medicine*, *67*, 28–36. Available from https://doi.org/10.1016/j.jflm.2019.07.010.

Glogan, D. R. N., Levitan, R. D. M. D., Brooks, D. E. M. D., & Gerkin, R. D. M. D. (2013). Unintentional use of mistaken insulin products: a retrospective review of poison center data. *Journal of Emergency Medicine*, *45*(4), 547–553. Available from https://doi.org/10.1016/j.jemermed.2013.01.032.

Hänsch, C. F., & De Roy, G. (1977). An extraordinary case: suicide with insulin in a grave dug by the victim himself. *Zeitschrift fur Rechtsmedizin. Journal of legal medicine*, *79*(4), 319. Retrieved from http://murdoch.summon.serialssolutions.com/2.0.0/link/0/eLvHCXMwtV1bS8MwFA7qfBBEvOKdvJeONm16EXwY6tQ30fnii6RpogVXx9YJ-us9yem2OlD0QShpSdlY852dfifJdw4hAWt77pxPEJkEYsSCMIhjLWKeszDXvi9C6PaZjCbZGew21ZkAe27r6n8BD30AvRHS_gH86ZdCB1yDCUALRgDtr8ygY5L4-V0MBMSYqb6VAOfpoXMgiVzgRO9mRDodwsCJRPn6y1BTM6M3IRvrOc9EfqRf-dpLMPqqggPB4WunL0eGhI6HM1Muv1H0XZdhps90U91TqV5kr-lV2nD8sRFqRq7DM-V84tThNeziYmfKCRZk0ddf4TZxuGLiAeNJ0tVo6pjSpseM4APWcDkkHfYpLSYTVTn66N5c0u75h0qf34cGqU1W693eLpGWUSDa-uO5OXthRGtoybtPfu0KW8fNzoYalHL11słaPHu0gqhtkQZWbZBUnWinqx7bITaekXxCmBuETWuNLDb60xhf-OVFCLLwV8afZOAV-K-NIa323S6170zq7cukyGK3kUuCkHEsIli7UnPE9LYNjAMTyh4lT6qeCpZ4JGlWRSM5nxxMtiiNmZAOosYNA52yFL5WupdglNVC54LCV4cQFxd5ZEMklFoFiWJxwC8z2yjePxOMBUKI84Tvvf9B-QlZlhHJKWhj-VOppW6jq2MHwCEe5LXg.

Iwase, H., Kobayashi, M., Nakajima, M., & Takatori, T. (2001). The ratio of insulin to C-peptide can be used to make a forensic diagnosis of exogenous insulin overdosage. *Forensic Science International*, *115*(1), 123–127. Available from https://doi.org/10.1016/S0379-0738(00)00298-X.

Johansen, N. J., & Christensen, M. B. (2018). A systematic review on insulin overdose cases: clinical course, complications and treatment options. *Basic & Clinical Pharmacology & Toxicology*, *122*(6), 650–659. Available from https://doi.org/10.1111/bcpt.12957.

Kernbach-Wighton, G., & Püschel, K. (1998). On the phenomenology of lethal applications of insulin. *Forensic Science International*, *93*(1), 61–73. Available from https://doi.org/10.1016/S0379-0738(98)00032-2.

Kuhn, B., & Cantrell, L. (2008). Unintentional overdose of insulin glargine. *American journal of Health-System Pharmacy*, *65*(6). Available from https://doi.org/10.2146/ajhp070602, 508-508.

Lutz, R., Pedal, I., Wetzel, C., & Mattern, R. (1997). Insulin injection sites: morphology and immunohistochemistry. *Forensic Science International*, *90*(1), 93–101. Available from https://doi.org/10.1016/S0379-0738(97)00153-9.

Marks, V. (2009). Murder by insulin: suspected, purported and proven—a review. *Drug Testing and Analysis*, *1*(4), 162–176. Available from https://doi.org/10.1002/dta.38.

Marks, V., & Richmond, C. (2008). Kenneth Barlow: the first documented case of murder by insulin. *Journal of the Royal Society of Medicine*, *101*(1), 19. Retrieved from http://murdoch.summon.serialssolutions.com/2.0.0/link/0/eLvHCXMwtV3dS8MwEA_qQHwRv78l72Mj69K0FRRkOPTZ7Xk0H4WBa4co4n_vXS9tZ2EwH3wpa7K-FJb_r9XK5-x1jw6Avei2dkAkjEo1M0GAw6zBwUimrFNwFA7gVFTtDGabapKK0Qlf_C3hoA-gxkfYP4NeDQgN8BhGAKwgBXDcSA593g-cKb8VXFcWRzcHo69rCfJacnLZrUvLpI2O4e0eb1AeprzFecRDyPFRhnxhK0zqnxzwgKrY-z81KgA0m8y98OeMRlQ1yv7wP8Yr3oXJIQkNEpXH6jpQo7EFAvVPxzFrLNr-qxYl0JqnMFSyWixIM3PkME7FBb4sxu-5C9vQFzPzj3uW96es262AiUrm9eBnXZ00yoXp71UyQR9aP0NprlDbH5IDt-_XmjwTrIdty-RHbrZb5mD14dDmhe8cBFl5iyxtsOWLLi4wTtlx_c4_tCZuOnyaj554viNGD_xZhtgy8DVSmrIFnJpJgncUmyDItdBpapxwoWLDIkhhJhsBUt-lARrFF-h2koNRpcMp28iJ354zL2BkJ-tvqVEkDXxKBhndNqFUkw8SJC3ZGM58tifVkVq3J5dqeK7bXiMg162TwDLmbujDXbbnsP5_TQhk.

McIntyre, A. S., Woolf, V. J., & Burnham, W. R. (1986). Local excision of subcutaneous fat in the management of insulin overdose. *The British journal of surgery*, *73*(7), 538. Retrieved from http://murdoch.summon.serialssolutions.com/2.0.0/link/0/eLvHCXMwtV3NS8MwFA_qEHYRRYff5C6VLf1IevAwZWOCNzd3HM0XDFw72Ab--b40aVMLih68hNKUQPt7fXlJfu_3EArJfT9o-QQR8phlQgiYMMzRG8l0FkW6nzJBeFqeu3uaqmf2tqir_wU83APoTSLtH8CvB4UbcA0mAC0YAbS_MoMXM1fdqQ9bSceEhps-dFzsICZUhv-psWzEdVzURxspIWI66YXjKYvOFMDR1nAIjhtRQntg0MqzLnT6_xT30O6zzongvhSDf_InUI4zh8rXnjsEobWYeS2rSqneuNIDFrfVXyvrTkkQ3sJVzKodr-a5c4w6IN7xlboZcGLOtViQsYTESt6NGPnS3p7KrHqKiv5FJsH1QezF73UcckJBkC4Oh57M-c-rHVlnev0UWHboDWkqMMPabH6MitGfDQonuC9lR-iiYlsrhCFhcaN5HFgCxe5hiQxR5Z85RDFlfInqHZeDR9mgSuLEYgwHvSQKoYfp1Ymmhe8EhDRE2-TVPOUC060ppxIoULCdRRqQhjP-hmRjMdUp1HIYk166CAvcnWOMBtENBGmEjwxaUJmYzmkLM1kwlgiM32BevbFF2urfbJwX-Tyu44r1PW2cY06Gv4jdVMX57otP_knXeBGzg.

Nikolic, S., Atanasijevic, T., & Popovic, V. (2006). A suicide by insulin injection: Case report. *Srpski arhiv za celokupno lekarstvo*, *134*(9–10), 444–447. Available from https://doi.org/10.2298/SARH0610444N.

Palmiere, C., Sabatasso, S., Torrent, C., Rey, F., Werner, D., & Bardy, D. (2015). Post-mortem determination of insulin using chemiluminescence enzyme immunoassay: preliminary results. *Drug Testing and Analysis*, *7*(9), 797–803. Available from https://doi.org/10.1002/dta.1775.

Russell, K. S., Stevens, J. R., & Stern, T. A. (2009). Insulin overdose among patients with diabetes: a readily available means of suicide. *Primary care companion to the Journal of clinical psychiatry*, *11*(5), 258–262. Available from https://doi.org/10.4088/PCC.09r00802.

Shibutani, Y., & Ogawa, C. (2000). Suicidal insulin overdose in a Type 1 diabetic patient: relation of serum insulin concentrations to the duration of hypoglycemia. *Journal of Diabetes and Its Complications*, *14*(1), 60–62. Available from https://doi.org/10.1016/S1056-8727(00)00057-X.

Smith, K. G. V. (1986). *A Manual of Forensic Entomology*. London: Trustees of the British Museum, Natural History and Cornell University Press.

Tong, F., Wu, R., Huang, W., Yang, Y., Zhang, L., Zhang, B., … Zhou, Y. (2017). Forensic aspects of homicides by insulin overdose. *Forensic Science International*, *278*, 9–15. Available from https://doi.org/10.1016/j.forsciint.2017.06.015.

CHAPTER 3

A homicide and a chat with a neighbour

Edda Emanuela Guareschi
Medical, Molecular and Forensic Sciences, College of Science, Health, Engineering and Education, Murdoch University, Murdoch, WA, Australia

ABSTRACT
During the investigation of a shooting homicide, a series of pelvic fractures was found in a young female victim. The cause of these fractures instigated a detailed investigation to establish their relationship, or otherwise, with the homicide. Pelvic fractures can involve any pelvic bones and achieve anatomical instability of the pelvic ring. They can be complicated by internal or external hemorrhages, related to lacerations of major blood vessels or organs, caused by sharp edges of dislocated bone fragments. These lacerations can be life-threatening by evolving into a rapidly fatal hemorrhagic shock. Most pelvic fractures result from high-energy injuries, typically in motor vehicle accidents and falls from a height. In falls from a height, a positive correlation between the level of the height and the seriousness of the injuries has been analysed in the scientific literature and established. Postmortem pelvic fractures are difficult to detect at the autopsy by reason of their anatomical location in the human body, thus the routine use of a non-contrast postmortem computed tomography (PMCT) before performing the conventional autopsy has been recommended since the late 2000s.

Keywords: Homicide; gunshot wounds; pelvic fractures; noncontrast postmortem computed tomography (PMCT); falls from a height

Even though any forensic pathologist would consider a call from the law enforcement as perfectly normal, especially when one is on duty, the kind of call that arrived in early April 2011 was particularly unwelcome, because the case was immediately presented as bleak and troublesome: a 24 years old woman had been killed by an older male acquaintance, who had then waited one week before turning himself in. During that week he apparently moved the body several times. Beyond cause, mode and manner of

Forensic Pathology Case Studies. DOI: https://doi.org/10.1016/B978-0-12-824294-0.00010-8

death, a peculiar investigation had to be launched in order to assess the time of death and the taphonomy changes on the body for the purpose of corroborating or negating the perpetrator's testimony.

After an hour drive through sleepy green hills and undulated fields, I finally arrived at an old and dilapidated farm house, where the police and its forensic staff had been conducting the crime scene investigation for a few hours. We all agreed that the scene did not feature anything really relevant, except a pit excavated in the property grounds. The pit was 1.8 m deep with a rectangular margin, it had been excavated by proper earth moving machinery and it contained a body wrapped in a blanket. The perpetrator, a 30-something years old man, had confessed his crime on that same Saturday morning and his story was so appalling that it was immediately believed, since it is hardly possible to make up such a horror. The preceding Sunday he and the victim, with whom he was apparently involved in a sentimental relationship, quarrelled about financial issues. He drove the victim to the farm house, which was his property but had been left uninhabited for years, parked the car, walked around it to the front the passenger's seat and fired two gunshots. He then buried the body in a manually dug shallow grave and left. Four days later, on Thursday, he drove back to the farm house, dug the body up, brought it inside the house, wrapped it in various layers of materials—the outer one a blanket—and left it there. Next day, on Friday, he drove back to the farm house again and went to visit a neighbour, casually asking for help to dig a hole and justifying it with the aim of burying some junk. They had a neighbourly chat, most likely very similar to many others they had had in the past, and they both headed off with the neighbour's mechanical excavator. During the short drive on the excavator, from the neighbour's property to the perpetrator's one, the police report mentions that the unaware neighbour cracked a joke, asking the perpetrator if he had to bury a body, and that joke was met by the perpetrator with a casual comment and a hearty laughter. Once the neighbour and the excavator were gone, the body was unceremoniously dumped in the pit, and the pit was filled with earth. The next day, Saturday, the perpetrator turned himself in.

At the crime scene, I examined the body superficially, which was wrapped in several layers of different materials and secured with duct tape, specifically a plastic sheet, two layers of nylon fabric and an old blanket. The body was only slightly bloated and in the chromatic stage of putrefaction, gunshot wounds in the head and thorax were evident. Before any other investigations, the body was cautiously unwrapped, transferred to a body bag and sent for a comprehensive CT scan, which detected two gunshot wound trajectories, both confirmed at the autopsy and both lethal. One bullet entered the head in the right parietal bone and exited from the left temporal region, with several skull fractures and massive cerebral damage, the other entered the thorax in the right mammary region, pierced the thorax wall and passed through the right lung, the right ventricle of the heart, the diaphragm muscle and the liver, and exited from the left flank, with structural damage to internal organs and extensive hemorrhage. The CT scan also revealed other, and rather unforeseen, lesions, such as two pelvic fractures, one of the left ilio-pubic branch, close to the pubic symphysis, and the other of both the right sacral ala and the right hemilamina of the first sacral vertebra (Fig. 3.1).

Pelvic fractures can involve any of the pelvic bones—ilium, ischium, pubis and sacrum—which with the anterior and posterior sacroiliac ligaments and fibrous joints form a ring. The pelvic ring is defined as disrupted when two or more fractures occur in different anatomic locations of the pelvis, and the consequence is anatomical instability. Pelvic fractures can be complicated by internal or external hemorrhages, generated by lacerations to major blood vessels or organs by sharp edges of dislocated bone fragments, and which can be life-threatening by evolving into a rapidly fatal hemorrhagic shock (Hussami, Grabherr, Meuli, & Schmidt, 2017; Scemama et al., 2015; Tosounidis & Giannoudis, 2013). The most common vascular injuries involve the external

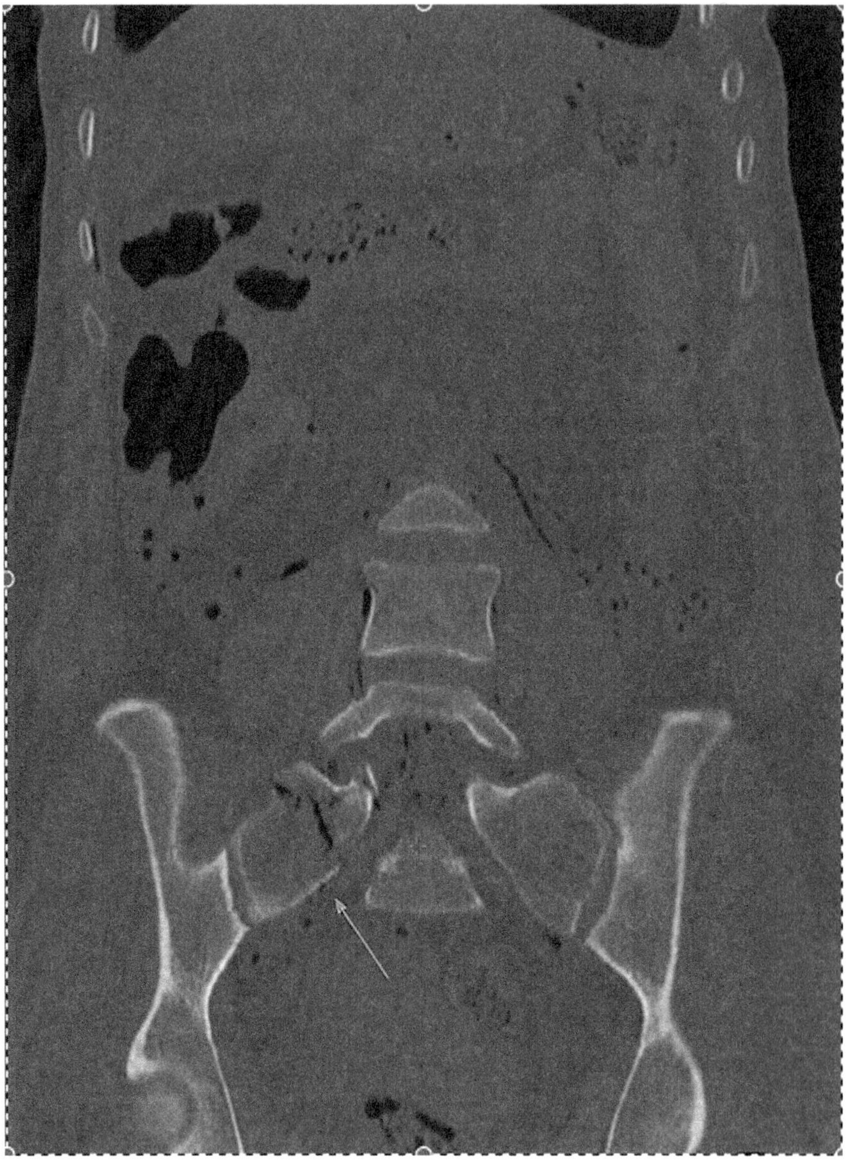

Figure 3.1 Pelvic fracture (arrow).

and internal iliac artery and the obturator artery (Kachlik et al., 2019). Most pelvic fractures result—in healthy individuals—from high-energy injuries, typically in motor vehicle accidents and falls from a height (Adams, Davis, Heidepriem, Alonso, & Alexander, 2002; de Bakker et al., 2018). In elderly individuals suffering from osteoporosis, low-energy injuries can generate pelvic fractures, as well (Bergeron et al., 2006). The diagnosis is clinical and involves radioimaging, X-rays and CT scan, where CT scan is more sensitive than X-rays. Stable pelvic fractures usually only require symptomatic treatment, whereas unstable fractures are treated by external or internal fixation. Critical hemorrhages and hemodynamic instability require angiographic embolization or emergency surgery.

The pelvic fractures found in the present case were not consistent with the dynamics of the confessed homicide. The absence of any suggestive finding, both at the external examination and at the autopsy, confirmed the lack of any physical trauma—other than gunshot wounds—to the victim. In fact, the analysis of the bullet trajectories, combined with evidence in the car, established the position of the victim as seated in the car when the perpetrator abruptly fired his weapon. The hypothesis of the perimortem (at or very close to the time of death) production of the pelvic fractures was thus eliminated, also with the support of the absence of any hemorrhagic infiltration in the pelvic soft tissues. The antemortem production was also ruled out, on the basis of the lack of any bone remodelling and the significant diastasis of the fracture of the right sacral ala, which would have been extremely painful and accompanied by hemorrhage/haematoma with serious locomotion impairment. The postmortem occurrence of the fractures, on the contrary, was substantiated by the lack of any vital reaction of the soft tissues surrounding the involved pelvic bones, and it would be consistent with the perpetrator's confession of having dumped the body in the pit five days after the homicide. Considering the depth of the pit and the possible use of machinery to lift and dump the body, the estimated height of the body fall was 2–3 m.

At the autopsy the pelvic fractures could have been overlooked, by reason of the lack of associated lesions, such as abdominal hemorrhages, and because the anatomic location is quite hard to access and dissect. Furthermore, confounding factors tend to increase in a decomposing body. Non-contrast postmortem computed tomography (PMCT) has been routinely used since the late 2000s, both as an aiding investigation tool for the conventional autopsy, and for initial injury screening before performing the autopsy. PMCT and autopsy present a different level of consistency between their findings, and the consistency ratio is based on the tissues, the pathologies examined and the anatomical locations in the human body. PMCT is more sensitive to gases, fluids and hard materials, either biological, like bone fractures, or inert, such as shards, bullets and small foreign bodies, whereas autopsy is more reliable for soft tissue-parenchymal organs injuries, lacerations by bullet tracks and incised wounds. PMCT with the injection of contrast medium (Angiographic PMCT, or PMCTA) is occasionally used in selected cases when lesions in the cardio-vascular system are suspected (Adelman et al., 2018; Jalalzadeh et al., 2015).

The last debatable issue in this case was the consistency of the observed postmortem pelvic fractures with so low a height as the one estimated for the fall of the body into the excavated pit, 2–3 m. In falls from height, a positive correlation exists between the level of the height and the seriousness of the injuries, and that correlation is mediated by the amount of energy which develops during the fall. That same energy—kinetic—is transformed into work with the sudden deceleration of the body at the moment of impact with the ground. Several literature studies report pelvic fractures as occurring in higher falls than the one estimated in the present case, such as 8.5 m (Weilemann, Thali, Kneubuehl, & Bolliger, 2008) or more (de Bakker et al., 2018). The correlation between height and injuries in falls has always been a classic topic in the forensic literature (Atanasijevic, Savic, Nikolic, & Djoki, 2005; Lau, Ooi, & Phoon, 1998). A reasonable explanation for the present case takes into account the slight build—hardly 50 kg of body weight—and the ethnicity of the victim, who had recently migrated to Italy from a developing country and might have had a history of nutritional imbalance, which led to an increased bone fragility.

The case was closed as a homicide, and the perpetrator testimony was corroborated by the overall findings, also with regards to the time of death, because the burial and/or wrapping of the body for most of the time before the recovery could clarify the slowing down of the decomposition process. The rest of the investigations panel listed toxicology on blood, which disclosed the presence of amphetamines and alcohol in the victim's system. Both findings, though, were heavily influenced by the chemistry of putrefaction. As a consequence, alcohol concentration was not considered reliable and the presence of amphetamines was completely ascribed to a putrefaction artefact. Genetic analysis on several biological samples from the victim led to the conclusion that she was spared any sexual involvement.

References

Adams, J. E., Davis, G. G., Heidepriem, R. R. W., Alonso, J. E., & Alexander, C. B. (2002). Analysis of the incidence of pelvic trauma in fatal automobile accidents. *The American Journal of Forensic Medicine and Pathology*, *23*(2), 132. Retrieved from http://murdoch.summon.serialssolutions.com/2.0.0/link/0/eLvHCXMwtV1LSwMxEA7Vgggivt-Se1nZTdJ9HDwUqejBk-1ZsnngwW57qP_fSWaTrRVFD16WkiyBZr6dzExmviGEs5s0WdMJWsCxMayEyVReVYUqNdixIrNCMAMHWhnYGXyaaq8XOkitpa7-l-BhDETvCmn_IPy4KAzAb4AAPAEE8PwVDFZJR5yN6ULrvo2oT3U2b6AoXJuI95l0kQ_re4nI9-V8Nq9BXwyk8q8j3VMwYiddNUqzSj0B9q9Lh1fxwh5ZCOTy9VPsfqTb-I6rzTaDr4QHbd1M1_bLk3EtwKn34OWYjY854YMYIxq9wR7iPZIL87frhoAG6xKvQoyz8iyaeF1jgl7m4OpiMmdQ3Fio3AKUrWjhDEOmK-JdzLx8MwY6iyEv8M-zayTcccoRss9gD5e3pkmmzxuk72qb3IkwfryPJgAXPtk1_hNHTduusOa-eDNmskd2W_-DjhAp-6RnmgOy9dQK7IDsYByXYnnaIXkIAKJzSwFANALIDSCAKAIIpqgHEO0ARCOAjsj0fjy5e0ja7huJyspcJGXNrarBIEylHnJT1dYWKXzATIINWOQSPF1uuahTo8H8MYZbWfEyV6kRSlVKsGOy2cwbc0qosLLQeihypkvX8Q5UvVaZLmrLyyEse-UZOcE9eFkix8hJ26_zbmQuy3YHnkvQtfLDmKnYBu_YC-QAgG2jO.

Adelman, A., Vasserman, M., Graziani, G., Kugel, C., Meir, K., Bdolah-Abram, T., & Krispin, A. (2018). Post-mortem computed tomography compared to medico-legal autopsy – pathologies in the torso and limbs. *Journal of Forensic Radiology and Imaging*, *12*, 43–49. Available from https://doi.org/10.1016/j.jofri.2017.12.002.

Atanasijevic, T. C., Savic, S. N., Nikolic, S. D., & Djoki, V. M. (2005). Frequency and severity of injuries in correlation with the height of fall. *Journal of Forensic Sciences*, *50*(3), 608. Retrieved from http://murdoch.summon.serialssolutions.com/2.0.0/link/0/eLvHCXMwtV1LS8NAEF6qvQgivt-yd4lk81iTgwdRix700upV9jXYWpPS

9v_j7G6SxoKiBy8h7ISFZD5mZicz8xESRxdhsGQTDBM6scFvpDW6OOAijjJxCaDS
UIHrJluUqXY6NVvaUunqfyke11D1tpH2D8pvNsUFvEcI4BVBgNdfwaA39bXSfswS
ukEzrYowhsXI0tW5elhlOTp8VVyVmUX0vLmsqX0UxHj8TRSLMa8tgVfnlSttQvRr-
jDrFbDhCx-tI1AdiPsKVVlZWVJL-uJSlRjvT_BV6Gr7bccVfhE1l8u2o9FTbL2aG-z1-
yVukiyrBVh8BY56D-sJU5jfl9kSbt-2zH0xb4TBuGVvuJkLMW1qcfDg1YogWR6EnT
_5ZujRruxHZuesfeqjmV6YInvsrpGtbmKzhv3voNZ6eM87qafT2TRzHk99h6ZTiopX
XBJtmoFESvPSC2SMcU22Td52ipbz3bIQ8NOCiCg9bgoCXQGhx4Q1vgoBYcFMFB
PTjsoxYcu2TQuxvc3AcVtUYwwSN2kCU61AwjwxwgSVIRopcBmUEqVZLHUuYSYi
1hzRXYFMAMswkxp6A5wfNMObZI6tFWZgDQmXIBFM6BWaSRGYqj3gmADiD
VMSGq0Oy7z_E68SPT3mtP9HRt5JjsrZAzAnp4ovMzGnD8HXmtPAJEZFe9Q.

Bergeron, E., Clement, J., Lavoie, A., Ratte, S., Bamvita, J.-M., Aumont, F., & Clas, D. (2006). A simple fall in the elderly: not so simple. *The Journal of Trauma: Injury, Infection, and Critical Care*, *60*(2), 268–273. Available from https://doi.org/10.1097/01.ta.0000197651.00482.c5.

de Bakker, H. M., Tijsterman, M., Kubat, B., Soerdjbalie-Maikoe, V., van Rijn, R. R., & de Bakker, B. S. (2018). Postmortem radiological case series of acetabular fractures after fatal aviation accidents. *Forensic Science, Medicine, and Pathology*, *14*(1), 62–69. Available from https://doi.org/10.1007/s12024-018-9946-1.

Hussami, M., Grabherr, S., Meuli, R. A., & Schmidt, S. (2017). Severe pelvic injury: vascular lesions detected by ante- and post-mortem contrast medium-enhanced CT and associations with pelvic fractures. *International Journal of Legal Medicine*, *131*(3), 731–738. Available from https://doi.org/10.1007/s00414-016-1503-4.

Jalalzadeh, H., Giannakopoulos, G. F., Berger, F. H., Fronczek, J., van de Goot, F. R. W., Reijnders, U. J., & Zuidema, W. P. (2015). Post-mortem imaging compared with autopsy in trauma victims – A systematic review. *Forensic Science International*, *257*, 29–48. Available from https://doi.org/10.1016/j.forsciint.2015.07.026.

Kachlik, D., Vobornik, T., Dzupa, V., Marvanova, Z., Toupal, O., Navara, E., … Baca, V. (2019). Where and what arteries are most likely injured with pelvic fractures? *Clinical Anatomy*, *32*(5), 682–688. Available from https://doi.org/10.1002/ca.23372.

Lau, G., Ooi, P. L., & Phoon, B. (1998). Fatal falls from a height: The use of mathematical models to estimate the height of fall from the injuries sustained. *Forensic Science International*, *93*(1), 33–44. Available from https://doi.org/10.1016/S0379-0738(98)00027-9.

Scemama, U., Dabadie, A., Varoquaux, A., Soussan, J., Gaudon, C., Louis, G., … Vidal, V. (2015). Pelvic trauma and vascular emergencies. *Diagnostic and Interventional Imaging*, *96*(7), 717–729. Available from https://doi.org/10.1016/j.diii.2015.05.004.

Tosounidis, T. I., & Giannoudis, P. V. (2013). Pelvic fractures presenting with haemodynamic instability: Treatment options and outcomes. *Surgeon, The*, *11*(6), 344–351. Available from https://doi.org/10.1016/j.surge.2013.07.004.

Weilemann, Y., Thali, M. J., Kneubuehl, B. P., & Bolliger, S. A. (2008). Correlation between skeletal trauma and energy in falls from great height detected by post-mortem multislice computed tomography (MSCT). *Forensic Science International*, *180*(2), 81–85. Available from https://doi.org/10.1016/j.forsciint.2008.07.003.

CHAPTER 4

An unfortunate family: an infant death by a rare disease

Edda Emanuela Guareschi[1] **and Letizia Gnetti**[2]
[1]Medical, Molecular and Forensic Sciences, College of Science, Health, Engineering and Education, Murdoch University, Murdoch, WA, Australia, [2]S.C. Anatomia e istologia patologica, Azienda Ospedaliero-Universitaria di Parma, Parma, Italy

ABSTRACT
The death of an infant, especially outside hospital or medical settings, immediately raises questions, if not patent suspicions, about child abuse. If child abuse is excluded, the differential diagnosis between sudden infant death syndrome (SIDS) and a huge number of congenital or acquired diseases might prove critically challenging for the pathologist. In this chapter, a case is presented where the overall circumstances could suggest child abuse, SIDS and/or medical malpractice. The post mortem clinical diagnosis, which led to assess the cause of death as natural by desquamative interstitial pneumonia (DIP), was achieved by histology. Medical malpractice was ruled out in conjunction with reference to an accurate analysis of hospital records. It is crucial and morally mandatory for both pathologists and law enforcement to remember that misdiagnoses/overdiagnoses in similar cases might hold dire and long lasting familiar, social and legal consequences.

Keywords: Desquamative interstitial pneumonia (DIP); sudden infant death syndrome (SIDS); child abuse; interstitial pneumonia

It is not an overstatement to say that just a handful of worse situations exist, for a forensic pathologist to find oneself in, than when physical abuse and medical malpractice may have taken place and are investigated in the same case. Especially distressing in this type of scenario is when the victim is a child. Compared to cases involving adults, the death of a child raises more stress and psychological pressure on the pathologist/s involved to ensure the greatest speed and accuracy of the investigation, as well as a higher pressure on the justice system to deliver a verdict

Forensic Pathology Case Studies. DOI: https://doi.org/10.1016/B978-0-12-824294-0.00006-6

on cause, mode and manner of death as soon as possible. Additionally, this type of case has the possibility of presenting a difficult situation for any medical investigator/s, as any misdiagnosis/overdiagnosis is deeply distressing and questions their medical ability, but may also have unfortunate effects on the delicate psychological balance of a family, which is already under considerable suffering and strain after the loss of a child. Furthermore, it is not uncommon, even once a case has been solved and concluded, that the family of the deceased child will not regain its usual relational dynamics and overall composure for some considerable time, if ever.

On a day of early February 2011, it was in the company of these gloomy thoughts that I strode towards the city courthouse, fending off the usual biting cold of northern Italy winter, the whole picture made even bleaker by the constantly uniform grey sky. The prosecutor and I were discussing the assignment of a case involving the death of a 2-months old infant boy. According to the police report, the mother had called the territorial medical emergency service one mid-morning because her son had had a sudden seizure and had stopped breathing. Unfortunately, the resuscitation procedures proved unsuccessful, and death was declared about one hour after the initial event. The situation was complicated by two previous facts, firstly the infant boy had been discharged from the hospital only a week before, and secondly the mother had recently lost another child, a three years old epileptic girl, who died after a seizure even though she was, apparently, on specific medication. The reason for the recent infant boy's hospitalization was that, nine days before death, his father had had to upend him upside down after bottle feeding, and repeatedly pat him on the back to achieve the expulsion of some milk, which was apparently obstructing the tiny airways. Admitted to the city university hospital with a diagnosis of acute idiopathic respiratory distress, the infant boy was thoroughly examined, and the negative results, after a comprehensive array of laboratory and instrumental tests allowed the physicians to discharge him on the basis of his apparent good health. A follow up study of the hospital records led to the elimination of all concerns about medical malpractice on the part of the hospital staff.

Although the hospital report seemed to exclude any evidence or suspicion of child abuse, the general context of this infant death was potentially unnerving. While I had not received any additional information regarding the deceased child's family, their situation was very familiar. I found it very easy to glue the pieces of the puzzle together by reading the police report with the wisdom of a born and bred local. The family's home zip code and a few other clues sprinkled here and there, despite being written in a professionally aseptic style, came together in a vivid picture of a working-class family with a rudimentary education, living in a remote village on the hills, probably in an unwelcoming house and most likely not in luxury. The addiction of a similar child death in the recent past of the family completed the recipe for a potential social tragedy.

This explains the indescribable relief of everyone working in, or allowed to, the autopsy room, when at the external examination the infant boy looked healthy, clean and well cared-for. His morphometrical measurements, comprising but not limited to head circumference, abdominal circumference and foot length, displayed a regular physical development, and both the external examination and the autopsy excluded any traumatic lesion. All organs were collected in toto and fixed in formaldehyde for further analysis and histology. The brain was oedematous, traces of milk were found in the proximal segment of the oesophagus, and the same milk filled the stomach lumen. The remaining organs appeared free from macroscopic alterations, with the exception of the lungs, which showed irregular areas of increased compactness, hepatization-like, oedema and bilateral subpleural petechiae. The outcome of lung histology, using tissue stained with the classical hematoxylin-eosin method, depicted the presence of micro-foci of bilateral desquamative alveolitis with bacterial colonies in bronchi, bronchioles and alveoli, plus emphysema, whereas other organs, like liver, spleen, adrenal glands and thymus, showed microscopic and aspecific signs of cellular hypoxia (vacuolization, congestion). The overall findings suggested an acute respiratory failure in the context of a chronic respiratory failure associated with desquamative interstitial pneumonia (DIP) as the cause of death. A regurgitation of milk might actually have triggered the acute respiratory failure. Toxicology was also performed on a blood sample and, as expected, delivered a negative outcome.

DIP is a rare lung disease (Ju, Ke, Zhong, Fang, & Li, 2017) which is even more rarely reported on children (Bressieux-Degueldre, Rotman, Hafen, Aubert, & Rochat, 2014; Gerkowicz, Rozynek, & Pietroń, 1976; Rosenow, O'Connell, & Harrison, 1970; Schneider, Nevius, & Brown, 1967). Its description as a defined nosological entity dates back to 1965 (Liebow, Steer, & Billingsley, 1965), because before then it was classified as a variant of interstitial pneumonia, and regarded as an early stage of idiopathic interstitial fibrosis. The disease is characterized by accumulation of macrophages, originally believed to be "desquamating alveolar epithelial cells," in alveolar lumens, with mild to moderate fibrotic thickening of alveolar septa, mild chronic interstitial inflammation and absence of hyaline membranes. In the adult, it has been linked to active or passive exposure to cigarette smoke and carries a favourable prognosis, whereas in children the mortality is much higher, having also recently been linked to mutations in genes involved in surfactant metabolism (Ischander, Fan, Farahmand, Langston, & Yazdani, 2014). The prevalence of DIP is not exactly known. The initial symptoms comprise dry cough, low-grade fever, dyspnea, lung rales, clubbing, cyanosis and, in children, growth retardation. The diagnosis is clinical and radiological, but eventually achieved by histology on lung biopsy (Tazelaar, Wright, & Churg, 2011) (Fig. 4.1A–E).

To date, no standard treatment has been developed, but antibiotics, daily oral corticosteroids, chloroquine and high dose intravenous corticosteroid pulses have been employed successfully. Lung transplantation may become the only choice if the medication treatment fails, although post-transplantation recurrences have been reported (Diken et al., 2019; Paul et al., 1999).

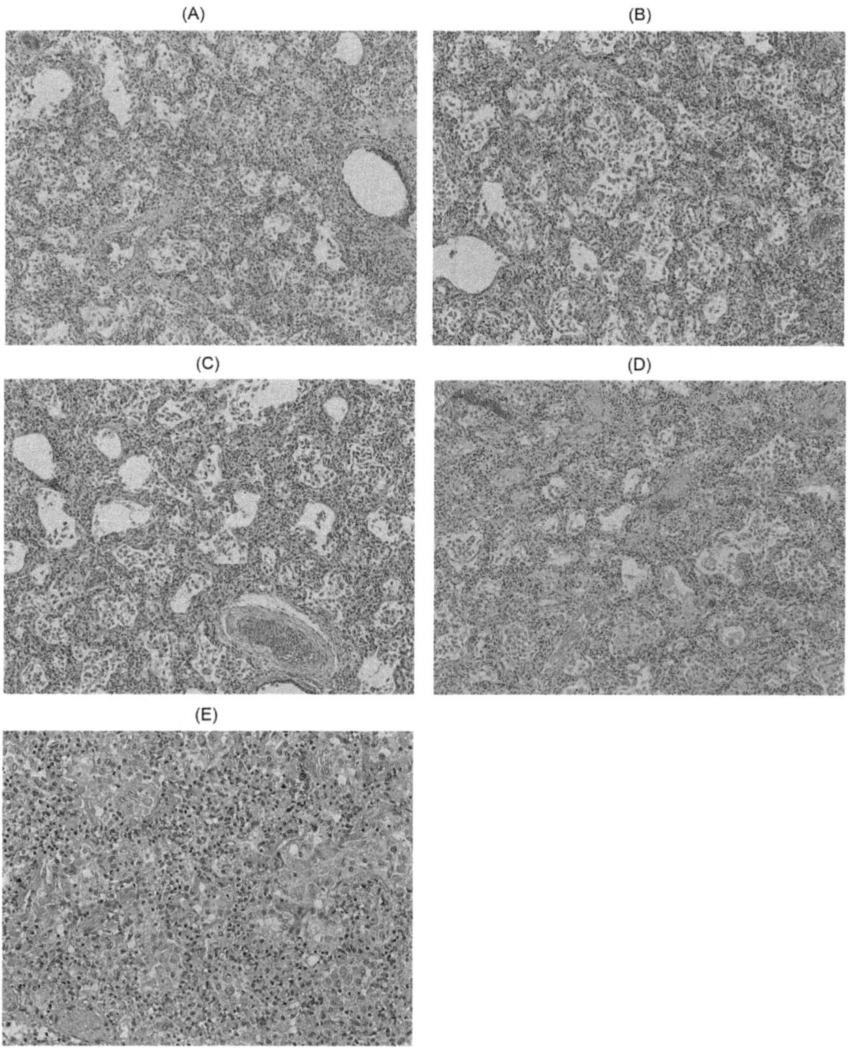

Figure 4.1 Desquamative Interstitial Pneumonia. Pneumocytes hyperplasia along alveolar septa and presence of numerous macrophages with eosinophilic cytoplasm, diffusely distributed along pulmonary acini within alveoli. The alveolar structure is preserved despite mild chronic interstitial inflammation. (H&E 4×, 10×, 20×).

In the past, interstitial pneumonia was not always distinguished from sudden infant death syndrome (SIDS), with subsequent confusion, diagnostic overlaps and scholarly debates. Today SIDS is defined as a sudden unexpected death in infancy, for which review of the history, a death scene investigation and a thorough autopsy provide no explanation, and it constitutes a differential diagnosis entity (Vege & Ole Rognum, 2004). The confusion may have aroused by reason that in SIDS hypoxia, which leads to asphyxia, plays a critical role.

As sad as it might possibly be, infants can die of natural death. Every time I think about this case, the in-between nine years seem to disappear, and I can almost feel the same grip of anxiety with stomach churning that I felt at the time when, walking from the city courthouse back to the morgue where the tiny body was waiting to be examined, I mentally listed the possible outcomes of the investigation, and none of them seemed reassuring, to say the least. Child abuse, SIDS related to socio-economic causes, medical malpractice, and/or their assorted combination would have made the life of everyone involved miserable for decades.

Child abuse (Barsness et al., 2003; Dubowitz & Bennett, 2007; Goodyear-Brown, 2012; Kaplan, 1986; Minns & Brown, 2005; Reece, 1993; Saukko & Knight, 2016) and SIDS (Bajanowski et al., 2006; Carlin & Moon, 2017; Dettmeyer & Kandolf, 2009; Horne, 2019; Keten & Okdemir, 2020; Krous et al., 2004; Thach, 2008) are, still and regrettably, much more common than one may assume. In my experience, a refresh on the topic, such as the one I did in these frantic hours, just before and just after operating on that tiny body, becomes mandatory to aid the average pathologist to exorcise the fear of misdiagnosis/overdiagnosis, with all its tragic consequences.

References

Bajanowski, T., Vege, Å., Byard, R. W., Krous, H. F., Arnestad, M., Bachs, L., … Rognum, T. O. (2006). Sudden infant death syndrome (SIDS)—Standardised investigations and classification: Recommendations. *Forensic Science International*, *165*(2), 129–143. Available from https://doi.org/10.1016/j.forsciint.2006.05.028.

Barsness, K. A., Cha, E.-S., Bensard, D. D., Calkins, C. M., Partrick, D. A., Karrer, F. M., & Strain, J. D. (2003). The positive predictive value of rib fractures as an indicator of nonaccidental trauma in children. *The Journal of Trauma: Injury, Infection, and Critical Care*, *54*(6), 1107–1110. Available from https://doi.org/10.1097/01.TA.0000068992.01030.A8.

Bressieux-Degueldre, S., Rotman, S., Hafen, G., Aubert, J.-D., & Rochat, I. (2014). Idiopathic desquamative interstitial pneumonia in a child: a case report. *BMC Research Notes*, *7*(1), 383-383. Available from https://doi.org/10.1186/1756-0500-7-383.

Carlin, R. F., & Moon, R. Y. (2017). Risk factors, protective factors, and current recommendations to reduce sudden infant death syndrome: a review. *JAMA Pediatrics*, *171*(2), 175. Retrieved from http://murdoch.summon.serialssolutions.com/2.0.0/link/0/eLvHCXMwtZ3JS8NAFMYHtSBexH2XuddIMklmMoKHUix66KXLuWR5A4JJi_T_xzdLFgKiHDKVryEMkN7yG_yzXvpm-8RErJH3-tpApeJCrMsUSqIVZaAwH3FVxKSLJZK5H7tzmDKVNvK3l7p6n-BxzFErw_S_gF-86M4gJ9xCeAVFwFef7UMZrp0fGKb6piI0foy6Hqhzqh-e147NemEtCzBNVsyBhAz7e8KKDJapVBSFOJApcLgcTh3jgf2hHvnn4Y64EVRH27qfiBNAD9OP12neMe3rTCert2Rf201_eH2B_deAvc6v6nxAKNfLOCJx5nT0lpsbcM-Vt6pYRzoD20Glw2RTGihMyAA12_95tuec3UxpF_WyeM-3z1B5y_kuGegDSSbNeJs0b-R07ByFuitj_cVeqmFCjsUROXS5Ah1ZqsdkB6oTsj911RCnpNJwqcP4QFu07RiCpQ4s7YGl2zW1YKkFSy1YasDSGuwTHVGL9YwsJy-L8avn-md4KRMi8HKmEpFCzEFALriQOYswvpVBLIBzH-nKNBKFirkMowxS7fVWcAz6Ch4lGePsnOxV6wouCcUn1U88AcwUQQQTAJQbCqYgYJsAZxFl6RS7snVptrEnKqr6H19_O3JCDdt3ckoHCRw7umj5e94bOF0AFVXE.

Dettmeyer, R. B., & Kandolf, R. (2009). Cardiomyopathies—misdiagnosed as sudden infant death syndrome (SIDS). *Forensic Science International*, *194*(1), e21–e24. Available from https://doi.org/10.1016/j.forsciint.2009.10.010.

Diken, Ö. E., Şengül, A., Beyan, A. C., Ayten, Ö., Mutlu, L. C., & Okutan, O. (2019). Desquamative interstitial pneumonia: Risk factors, laboratory and bronchoalveolar lavage findings, radiological and histopathological examination, clinical features, treatment and prognosis. *Experimental and Therapeutic Medicine*, *17*(1), 587–595. Available from https://doi.org/10.3892/etm.2018.7030.

Dubowitz, H. P., & Bennett, S. F. (2007). Physical abuse and neglect of children. *Lancet, The*, *369*(9576), 1891–1899. Available from https://doi.org/10.1016/S0140-6736(07)60856-3.

Gerkowicz, T., Rozynek, M., & Pietroń, K. (1976). Interstitial desquamative pneumonia in children. *Pediatria Polska*, *51*(2), 161. Retrieved from http://murdoch.summon.serialssolutions.com/2.0.0/link/0/eLvHCXMwtV1LS8NAEB7UIvQiihZflVx6jObZNAcPUqx6E63nkscEQswm9oHYX-9sNo9tUNSDlyVkYXfZbxhmh5nvAzCNS01t-QR0uGCaE2poBYajOV7kmyObQm89ojdSYFXsDEWZaiMw2Cpd_S_g6R9Bzxtp_wB-vSj9oG8yARrJCGj8lRkUGT9eD8Az4yEu3lZeKri-c4YrOkbs8ZRH1dMtx6qViofHlRwWSe2_73CeZO9xsN6osX7K1h8Mk40E62OMy3k2GNuDkdWkVEPRdOfUZcmN3zR11XQF7VDlN21dsg9DcoK6oFeXbjdPi-ulYGroGj9PthiwqxlOhp6GcbC8Rqa-PG9Dh_cVFa-Fh0mdWNO4uLsmlBLLU3dht1yj9XgogojpPuyV0b9yI3A6gK389RCuZIwUGSOlxkiJmVJhdAT9ye10fK-KPWa5IAyZlZsbPdhhGcNjUIzQtdCKKNbyKb7SfNdEj1PBmY6PoWe5J9D7eo3T7ybOoNsgdw6diAwY-7Uq1kVxSZ_EUhz5.

Goodyear-Brown, P. (2012). In N. J. Hoboken (Ed.), *Handbook of child sexual abuse: identification, assessment, and treatment* (1. Aufl.;1st ed.). John Wiley & Sons.

Horne, R. S. C. (2019). Sudden infant death syndrome: current perspectives. *Internal Medicine Journal*, *49*(4), 433–438. Available from https://doi.org/10.1111/imj.14248.

Ischander, M., Fan, L. L., Farahmand, V., Langston, C., & Yazdani, S. (2014). Desquamative interstitial pneumonia in a child related to cigarette smoke. *Pediatric Pulmonology*, *49*(3), E56–E58. Available from https://doi.org/10.1002/ppul.22812.

Ju, Y., Ke, H. X., Zhong, X. F., Fang, F., & Li, Y. M. (2017). Desquamative interstitial pneumonia: report of one case and review of literature. *Zhonghua jie he he hu xi za zhi = Zhonghua jiehe he huxi zazhi = Chinese Journal of Tuberculosis and Respiratory Diseases*, *40*(10), 760. Retrieved from http://murdoch.summon.serialssolutions.com/2.0.0/link/0/eLvHCXMwtV3NS8MwFA_TXbyI4vfHyMVTmXT9WDfBg6hFb4IThpeRtqmtbO2cK8j-et9L2iYUhnoQRhlJSNO-X19ekvd-jxDbujS7DZ2AIZTmwAlCm6EF3rM4s91gEHmMcc-OwoqdQbiptlpVCrqG6-p_CR7KQPQYSPsH4dedQgH8BwjAFUAA11_BANaVHwWbSXpv5IZYoHMAbpPPM17AMFKRnEceHaDlmGfoCfYpTxVUYMu0pl_Wz-dnXJM_ekoIZ7ykHm1P8CuMrNVbMWCWpcWHfGXqbqoloUTXAFN4cbqiRWCyL-gC_CYpojXYociPIIKM-UlO9joeYRMXWI6dQYqz3x0u14rNyY_XKb3Nd3PWAmFU4kmqIWrmBDSYRUaXJJ_FQh1tT0sieTFmgCn8-ExK2h6SLl0M-1DVruugop2mdRGi6vedZ9ed4gbYx2EmuYR19Zpj08sq0tR1gHeqBbncpocCzTlVGb5WMhSXV5h8aCRxg-ox2yXa5Y6I3E1i5prZI98qTjiuq4ojWurqhEFc1jCqiiiCoKwqQSVVisULVPOv796PahKwcx-mUsWlEk1POuAbGbQyxGhgR1ZMQ-YOwj7Th-MR7PPnV7suHFgRbFpHpPDNZ2crK05JVtK_mekHcOHyc_rbF8d8Zq_AXjfZbo.

Kaplan, J. M. (1986). Pseudoabuse--the misdiagnosis of child abuse. *Journal of Forensic Sciences*, *31*(4), 1420. Retrieved from http://murdoch.summon.serialssolutions.com/2.0.0/link/0/eLvHCXMwtV3dS8MwEA_qEAYifuI3fZ8dS5Mm6YMPIg71SXB7Hm1yAcF1g23_v5ek60phqA--hJKEQO53vdwl90EIS_qDuCUT7EAVqWQ8y5lRmTQ8BQE0M1nBrUp1ts7O4N1UN5UPW66r_wU89iH0LpD2D-DXi2IHfiMLYItMgO2v2OB9ASszy4vVAuLYKZmIqwnudSETiY_m7vkJWxRVVGudl7vuVafl5vknn3-F-9O36lLVhHg6JWpHtKY7P6WhFHQfKimYCmdYZk0xyWiDHXhD5lHuw9mWDWrOp56cTLoyZurHwVbG6_WIS34-NZ96-QBlPP7YJR0XR-Stg9dhfdwKKug6JbzbR5fsVwu0LAWvMYyOyGFFwegxgHJMdqA8IQfhnjQK4V-n5L4NUNQEKJrZyAMU-QlnZDx8Hj29xFUFizinaInGiVEGdT4FihtptEgTqY1FFXgANheAZNbS8iKlhXt-NTnavraQXDADOZqikJyTvXJWwgWJUFACwx9nwDhwBlqBTplxr54iUVTKS3IeNjuZhzQlk4oKV9sGrkl3wxA3pGOR5eG2rqN158n8DXFtJvU.

Keten, A., & Okdemir, E. (2020). Sudden infant death syndrome. *American Journal of Forensic Medicine and Pathology*, *41*(2), 141. Available from https://doi.org/10.1097/paf.0000000000000551.

Krous, H. F., Beckwith, J. B., Byard, R. W., Rognum, T. O., Bajanowski, T., Corey, T., … Mitchell, E. A. (2004). Sudden infant death syndrome and unclassified sudden infant deaths: a definitional and diagnostic approach. *Pediatrics*, *114*(1), 234–238. Available from https://doi.org/10.1542/peds.114.1.234.

Liebow, A. A., Steer, A., & Billingsley, J. G. (1965). Desquamative interstitial pneumonia. *The American Journal of Medicine*, *39*, 369–404. Available from https://doi.org/10.1016/0002-9343(65)90206-8.

Minns, R. A., & Brown, J. K. (2005). *Shaking and other non-accidental head injuries in children* (Vol. no. 162). London: Mac Keith.

Paul, K., Klettke, U., Moldenhauer, J., Muller, K. M., Kleinau, I., Magdorf, K., & Wahn, U. (1999). Increasing dose of methylprednisolone pulse therapy treats desquamative interstitial pneumonia in a child. *European Respiratory Journal*, *14*(6), 1429–1432. Available from https://doi.org/10.1183/09031936.99.14614299.

Reece, R. M. (1993). Fatal child abuse and sudden infant death syndrome: a critical diagnostic decision. *Pediatrics*, *91*(2), 423–429. Retrieved from https://pediatrics.aappublications.org/content/pediatrics/91/2/423.full.pdf.

Rosenow, R. E. C., O'Connell, E. C., & Harrison, J. E. G. (1970). Desquamative interstitial pneumonia in children. Report of two cases. *American Journal of Diseases of Children (1960)*, *120*(4), 344. Retrieved from http://murdoch.summon.serialssolutions.com/2.0.0/link/0/eLvHCXMwtV07T8MwELYKFagL4lXxlneUKrHT2BkYEFCVgYl2rhzHkTo0L

YWKv8_5EdeKhICBJYpsyUpyX85357vvEKJkEEctnUArnirBSVWqNBEyKwBIhdBsY-ZQrWiUNO4NJU-10GsG3Ulf_S_AwBqLXhbR_EL5fFAbgHiAAVwABXH8FA_Ar3z ZiYem9NTfEWicH6DD5qlYbeIy50CGPpqZ74CxykzrwubyVsMm9hwasP-EJKCfcIY9J CvHF4ZoACvyWINKgmzjW9iiJ2oT6p22MtpV0E8yMxdr0STR4s8U5riFYaav3WOzT3-kIFnBPTQR22HzNGKNOHM04NN0qZxAH60kDFUssXGchutTDCA08X3G3642SL-X7uZ0VTri3IuP-5UHU1fd1BXVy0ZX-R55Dd3Srj3qPR79NCeW6Dllxj7ZHKIDpxjge8t BI5QR9XHaP_FpU6coMcQCThEAvZIgGHskYAtEvCywoAEbJBwiqajp8nDOHItNC-KRJCyJhlQz7guRMF7A75fKIlOcijJjpJBFXkqRVISlQ6LDWWD-lqxMuRyKXCqaSBq TPtqtl7U6Qxg2xYoJkgkegwmdV7xMixzWUplSFNzSc9S37z9bWZ6UmfswF99NXKLeF iNXqFvBP6eufSOvG_PlvwBuGlJk.

Saukko, P. J. A., & Knight, B. A. (2016). *Knight's forensic pathology* (Fourth ed.). Boca Raton: CRC Press.

Schneider, R. M., Nevius, D. B., & Brown, H. Z. (1967). Desquamative interstitial pneumonia in a four-year-old child. *The New England Journal of Medicine*, *277*(20), 1056. Retrieved from http://murdoch.summon.serialssolutions.com/2.0.0/link/0/eLvHCXMwtV1 LS8QwEA7qouxFfC2-6V0ibZqmLehBxGU96GV3z0vaZlBwu6vYg__eSZNtY0HRg5dS SEhqa-abTmck8CAnZpU87MgF8iGXGc6FCKbIskFLG-CwXPqgiVGpVnaEOU21j2ju hq_8FPI4h9DqR9g_gN4viAN4jC-AVmQCvv2IDtCtfKzk35b11bYg3HRyg3eTLUlX4Gs Gs9SuzzkBeBq9AO3TxcvhcnxdhXXiY2FtE0_3IoT3eP5cf5U6upZJnK7dbc-4j-4Mlp72-u5 cQOM7BlJYVLyULAGprd0K1Wth878U1aCNKSc-8KVtMx2bDEsxXxHcKKaJ1yJjlR czmtM0N5KI9PW58fJTtns1YyuoD5HMrxfq5JOx-ukp5ORahPjfugUGrOGkt1Jn2zaBTr mRq12THbItrUXvBuD7C5ZU-Ue2XqwJN8nVy7Anguw1wCMw570vgDs1QAfkOnwon bnI7orYjBs1RzeNUxRFAIKDIZYJ2J-pmkQ9pEqtIpIXiDFCBDHImIOSxUIrl-JHVKU AoprMkSdmAbJSLUh0ST7EsRtWkkBAKXviBjCLgKQgBOar0MRyRgdn3bGnKnsws QY6_mzgh_ZY7TkkP8BNSZ01frvOa4p9x2ESB.

Tazelaar, H. D., Wright, J. L., & Churg, A. (2011). Desquamative interstitial pneumonia. *Histopathology*, *58*(4), 509–516. Available from https://doi.org/10.1111/j.1365-2559.2010.03649.x.

Thach, B. (2008). Tragic and sudden death. *Potential and proven mechanisms causing sudden infant death syndrome. EMBO reports*, *9*(2), 114–118. Available from https://doi.org/10.1038/sj.embor.7401163.

Vege, A., & Ole Rognum, T. (2004). Sudden infant death syndrome, infection and inflammatory responses. *FEMS Immunology and Medical Microbiology*, *42*(1), 3. Retrieved from http://murdoch.summon.serialssolutions.com/2.0.0/link/0/eLvHCXMwtV3NS8MwF FA_qULyIzu8vcp8dbZqmycHDlIkevLhNvI20TWVguzE_wP_el6ZNZ0XRg5dQGgj0_V 4fecnv_R5CPum6TiMmxComNGK-VqsjQioZcpYwGgruhdxLo0qdoaCp1gXYDerqfwE P7wB6XUj7B_DtovACnsEFYAQngPFXbjB41ZFFc67AhJ1Eb_isSoE2b0XGyksZphQ8-JDM373NDny1JhlUrzz5k_hNdVFKLN2XlZU82qVWdKiDvlend3nvWVeP1ka7q3E0f-c9NkeTidP6nJ26cDCGoZVvYkkXCHEyPj2FVlHA2pw0TwsBhoKfniUCZq-ouxHOw3 ywo0IBiTwDet8n6ebUhm2yktn56BCV7OVe6MBsuopSuRivzi5qounxWmUqn6jqJVk1m-hkWwUm47hJtooswXcM7huoSWVt9Gq6R_63kZrtyUzYhtdGKCxARoXQOMK6DNs-YcYAGF6EGVuYd9Doqj-8vHbK_hhODD-S7wSw2SJS6aNE5lIZQ_D1YO_BNG2Usk hqqUkRKDdMFGeCeJJFCUkFJOSplFHok120kk9ztY9wqggPwigQkRSU-YRLV3mC-7BKpBUBD9CescN4ZkRQxpWFDr-dOULrtbsco1YKv5Q6sX26TgsQPgB-FEkY.

SECTION 2

Casework of Forensic Anthropology

CHAPTER 5

A specific identification from mixed skeletal remains in a cemetery setting

Edda Emanuela Guareschi

Medical, Molecular and Forensic Sciences, College of Science, Health, Engineering and Education, Murdoch University, Murdoch, WA, Australia

ABSTRACT

The exhumation of a female toddler girl in 1992 triggered off a long judicial litigation about an alleged commingling of skeletal remains in a modern cemetery setting. The examination of the skeletal remains was conducted using the scientific principles, methodology and practice of forensic anthropology and forensic genetics. Some elements in the skeletal assemblage were easily recognizable as human, and were labelled by morphology, whereas others were fragmented. All bones and fragments were dry and odourless, and most, but not all, showed small size and developmental juvenile morphology. Representative bones of both the juvenile individual and other older individuals were selected for genetic analysis, and compared to the DNA of both the toddler's parents. The outcome of the combined examination confirmed the commingling of skeletal remains. The case exemplifies how anthropology is a useful forensic tool when dealing with juvenile osteology, posthumous genetic identification and bioarchaeology in modern cemetery settings, especially when unusual taphonomic alterations are observable.

Keywords: Juvenile osteology; posthumous genetic identification; documented skeletal collections; bioarchaeology; cemetery taphonomy

During 1953 in a small town in Italy's north-west, in the wake of the misery and ravages of World War II, vivid in the memory of its inhabitants, a young couple of bereaved parents buried their toddler daughter, who died of natural causes, in the local cemetery. Thirty-nine years went by, during which it was only possible to speculate about how many times they visited the tiny tomb, until 1992, when an exhumation was scheduled. The aging father decided to be present at the exhumation, and he witnessed

Forensic Pathology Case Studies. DOI: https://doi.org/10.1016/B978-0-12-824294-0.00005-4

the minute skeleton being transferred into a metal case, which was then entombed. Another seven years passed, and in 1999 the metal case—which contained the toddler's skeletal remains—was moved to a family vault, which was expected to be its final resting place. In the last move, the metal case was reopened and the father was dismayed by its contents: too many bones lay mixed on its bottom, many were fragmented and some were just too big to belong to his daughter. A judicial litigation then began between the shocked parents and the cemetery management. Perhaps it is by reason of that litigation that in 2003, in the course of maintenance works to the family vault, the metal case was once again reopened and found, in the father's words, "partially emptied". In 2005, the judge appointed a forensic anthropologist and a forensic geneticist to examine the contents of the metal case. The aim was to identify the human skeletal remains, and determine both the presence of the remains of the toddler girl and the presence of remains of some other individuals.

As the appointed forensic anthropologist, I was assigned the task to analyse and classify the skeletal remains commingled inside the metal case (Fig. 5.1).

Whole bones were easily recognizable as human and could be labelled by morphology. Others were heavily and irregularly fragmented, to the point of being unrecognizable. They were all

Figure 5.1 Contents of the metal case in 2005.

dry, odourless and lacking any soft tissue residuals. Some presented traces of rust, most likely due to percolation from the metal of the containing case. A few soft brushes, a passage under tap water and some fine mesh sieving were all the preparation the bones and the fragments needed prior to inspection. I then separated the recognizable bones from the fragments, and assigned the bones anatomical locations, summarized in Table 5.1.

Most bones were of a small size and reflected developmental juvenile morphology. Unfortunately, time and budgetary constraints—two constant companions of experts in judicial cases—did not allow a thorough examination of every single bone, thus

Table 5.1 Recognizable skeletal elements contained in the metal case.

Anatomical location	Skeletal elements
Head and masticatory apparatus	R and L temporal bone: petrous part
	L temporal bone: temporomandibular joint
	Occipital bone: squamous part
	Occipital bone: basilar part
	Occipital bone: lateral parts
	R and L parietal bone
	Frontal bone
	Mandible, with three deciduous teeth
	Left hemimaxilla with two deciduous teeth and two dental germs
	Ten loose teeth
Pectoral girdle and upper limbs	R and L clavicle
	R and L scapula
	R humerus
	R and L ulna
	R and L radius
	Distal epiphysis of humerus
Pelvic girdle and lower limbs	R and L ilium
	R and L femur
	R fibula
Vertebral column	Seventeen vertebral bodies

Figure 5.2 Juvenile mandible.

Figure 5.3 Juvenile left hemimaxilla.

I selected the three more representative bones in an obvious developmental growth stage for an age estimation, which could potentially confirm the toddler's age of 32 months. Furthermore, I chose three bones I deemed representative of an older age, in order to establish not only their unauthorized presence in the metal case, but also to achieve a rough estimate of the number of other represented individuals. These included the basilar part of an occipital bone, a juvenile mandible (Fig. 5.2) and a juvenile left hemimaxilla (Fig. 5.3), selected for the developmental age assessment.

The basilar part was measured (Fazekas & Kósa, 1978; Redfield, 1970), and the measurements of height (22 mm) and length (24 mm) were applied to a table adapted by Scheuer and MacLaughlin-Black (1994). They were consistent with an individual of 2 years and 6 months of age. The small mandible had three deciduous teeth, two erupted first molars (R and L, or 84 and 74 according to Zsigmondy system) and one second molar (L, or 75) beginning eruption. The left hemimaxilla had two erupted molars (first and second, 64 and 65) and two included dental germs in the front. According to most tables available in literature (Lysell, Magnusson, & Thailander, 1962; Ubelaker, 1978), it was possible to classify all teeth as belonging to a 2 years ± 8 months old individual. With regards to the "foreign" bones, the size alone of a squamous part (Fig. 5.4) and two lateral parts of an occipital bone revealed older individual/s.

In the squamous part of the occipital bone the ossification process starts from different cores which join during foetal life to form the four main parts of the occipital bone: one squamous, two lateral and one basilar parts. Marks of the vascular and nervous grooves progressively appear on the intracranial surface during the perinatal period, but never before 18 months of age. These increase quickly up to 4 years and settle between 7 and 9 years of age (Davidhoff, 1936; Macauly, 1951). The lateral parts of the occipital bone were assigned to an older individual solely based

Figure 5.4 Squamous part of an occipital bone.

on a dimensional criterion. Finally, I isolated a distal epiphysis of a humerus, in which the almost complete stage of maturation suggested an older age rather than a toddler's (Fig. 5.5).

In fact, in the humerus the four ossification cores, which give rise to distal humeral epiphysis (capitulum, medial epicondyle, trochlea and lateral epicondyle), appear at different ages (between 6 months and 10 years), and start fusing at about 10 years of age in females and 12 years of age in males; the fusion is then completed by 13–16 years of age, with differences between males and females.

Following the anthropological assessment, some bones were selected for genetic analysis (Table 5.2) and compared to the DNA of both parents, obtained through a salivary swab.

The results of the genetic analysis are summarized in Table 5.3.

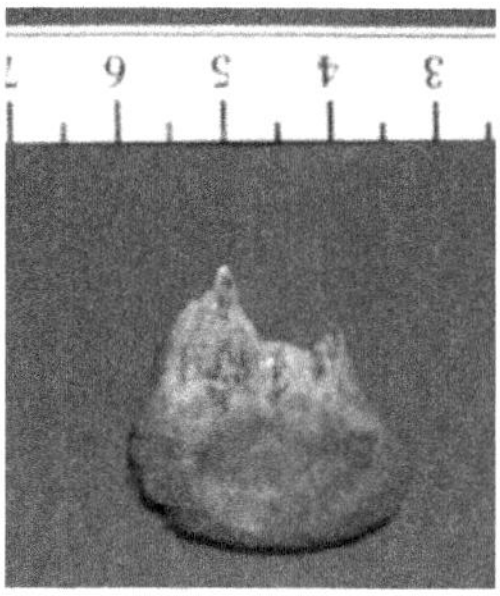

Figure 5.5 Distal epiphysis of a humerus.

Table 5.2 Skeletal elements selected for genetic analysis on the basis of the results from the anthropological assessment.

Skeletal element selected for genetic analysis	Results from anthropological assessment
Occipital bone, lateral parts	Unknown older individual
Occipital bones squamous part	Unknown older individual
R clavicle	Toddler girl
Distal epiphysis of humerus	Unknown older individual
R and L ilium	Toddler girl

Table 5.3 Results of the genetic analysis.

Sample subjected to genetic analysis	Result
Occipital bone lateral parts	No scientifically interpretable result
Occipital bone squamous part	
Distal epiphysis of humerus	Mixed male + female genetic profile
L and R ilium and R clavicle	Mixed and partial male + female genetic profile, some compatibilities with the comparing sample obtained from the mother

Aside from unusable skeletal material, such as bone fragments and bones which did not yield any scientifically interpretable results due to the lack of sufficient genetic material, like the occipital bone squamous part and the lateral parts, and considering the limitations of a 2005 genetic analysis with no certain sample from the toddler girl and confounded by contamination, both the anthropological and genetic assessments showed that most of the toddler girl's skeletal remains were actually stored in the metal case, where they had been placed after the 1992 exhumation. However, the same metal case also hosted a few "foreign" skeletal remains, which had belonged to at least two unknown individuals, a male and a female. These results suggested a reasonable reconstruction of the events which took place between 1992, the year of the first exhumation, and 2003, when the metal case was sealed for the last time. Most likely, after the 1992 exhumation some different skeletal remains were added to the toddler's ones in the metal case. After its reopening in 1999 the father complained about the excessive number and the size of some of the bones contained in the metal case, and issued a judicial litigation. As a consequence most of the bones in excess were removed from the metal case, but a few were left behind. In fact, at the following reopening, in 2003, the father described the metal case as "partially emptied", and that same situation persisted and was recorded at the time of my assignment, in 2005.

This case offered the opportunity to meditate on the application of the scientific principles and methodology of anthropology in three distinct disciplines which can occasionally acquire a forensic turn: juvenile osteology, posthumous genetic identification and bioarchaeology in modern cemetery settings. Juvenile osteology is not only complex, requiring extensive knowledge and experience, but it is mostly applied in archaeological and physical anthropology contexts (Brothwell, 1981; Krogman & Iscan, 1986; Molleson, 1986; Ortner, 2002; Waldron, 2009), extremely rarely in a small city forensic pathology practice. Therefore, the presented case highlights the need, for forensic anthropologists, to refer to the available literature that deals with the foetal and juvenile human skeleton with a straightforward and practical approach (Scheuer & Black, 2000). Furthermore, the resort to macro-anatomy, with the aim of selecting skeletal elements for genetic analysis, is a reminder of the still current and relevant role of macro-anatomy as a complement to newer biochemical and molecular approaches to biological studies, such as DNA analysis. DNA analysis was actually implemented in this case, where it typically exemplified a posthumous genetic identification (Edson, Ross, Coble, Parsons, & Barritt, 2004; Rocchi, Presciuttini, Chiti, Pierotti, & Spinetti, 2019; Stray & Shewale, 2010; van den Berge, Wiskerke, Gerretsen, Tabak, & Sijen, 2016), the comprehensive definition of paternity and parentage disputes involving deceased people, which are becoming more and more common in both civil and criminal contexts. Finally, the forensic application of the employment of forensic anthropologists in modern cemetery settings is not always necessarily immediate -although in perspective-, typical examples are the achievement of documented skeletal collections as references for studies in bioarchaeology and human skeletal biology (Alemán et al., 2012; Cattaneo et al., 2018; Ferreira et al., 2014; Katzenberg & Saunders, 2008; Kranioti, İşcan, & Michalodimitrakis, 2008; Ubelaker, 2014; Zvelebil & Weber, 2013), and the analysis of decomposition and taphonomy of human remains (Guareschi, Dadour, & Magni, 2019; Haglund & Sorg, 1997; Haglund & Sorg, 2002; Pokines & Symes, 2014; Sledzik & Willcox, 2009).

References

Alemán, I., Irurita, J., Valencia, A. R., Martínez, A., López-Lázaro, S., Viciano, J., & Botella, M. C. (2012). Brief communication: The Granada osteological collection of identified infants and young children. *American Journal of Physical Anthropology, 149* (4), 606–610. Available from https://doi.org/10.1002/ajpa.22165.

Brothwell, D. R. (1981). *Digging up bones: the excavation, treatment, and study of human skeletal remains*. Cornell University Press.

Cattaneo, C., Mazzarelli, D., Cappella, A., Castoldi, E., Mattia, M., Poppa, P., ... Biehler-Gomez, L. (2018). A modern documented Italian identified skeletal collection of 2127 skeletons: the CAL Milano Cemetery Skeletal Collection. *Forensic Science International, 287*, 219.e211–219.e215. Available from https://doi.org/10.1016/j.forsciint.2018.03.041.

Davidhoff, L. M. (1936). Convolutional digitations seen in roentgenograms of immature human skull. *Bulletin of the Neurological Institute of New York, 5*, 61–71.

Edson, S. M., Ross, J. P., Coble, M. D., Parsons, T. J., & Barritt, S. M. (2004). Naming the dead - confronting the realities of rapid identification of degraded skeletal remains. *Forensic Science Review, 16*(1), 63–90.

Fazekas, I. G., & Kósa, S. F. (1978). *Forensic fetal osteology*. Budapest: Akadémiai Kiadó.

Ferreira, M. T., Vicente, R., Navega, D., Gonçalves, D., Curate, F., & Cunha, E. (2014). A new forensic collection housed at the University of Coimbra, Portugal: The 21st century identified skeletal collection. *Forensic Science International, 245*, 202.e201–202.e205. Available from https://doi.org/10.1016/j.forsciint.2014.09.021.

Guareschi, E., Dadour, I. R., & Magni, P. A. (2019). Taphonomic examination of inhumed and entombed remains in Parma Cemeteries, Italy. *Global Journal of Forensic Science & Medicine, 1*(4), Retrieved from GJFSM.MS.ID.000518.

Haglund, W. D., & Sorg, M. (1997). *Forensic taphonomy the postmortem fate of human remains*. CRC Press.

Haglund, W. D., & Sorg, M. (2002). *Advances in forensic taphonomy (method, theory and archaeological perspectives)*. CRC Press.

Katzenberg, M. A., & Saunders, S. R. (2008). *Biological anthropology of the human skeleton*. Hoboken: Wiley-Liss.

Kranioti, E. F., İşcan, M. Y., & Michalodimitrakis, M. (2008). Craniometric analysis of the modern Cretan population. *Forensic Science International, 180*(2), 110.e111–110.e115. Available from https://doi.org/10.1016/j.forsciint.2008.06.018.

Krogman, W. M., & Iscan, M. Y. (1986). *The Human skeleton in forensic medicine*. Springfield Illinois USA: Charles Thomas Publisher.

Lysell, L., Magnusson, B., & Thailander, B. (1962). Time and order or eruption of the primary teeth: a longitudinal study. *Odontologisk Revy, 13*, 217–234.

Macauly, D. (1951). Digital markings in radiographs of the skull in children. *British Journal of Radiology, 24*, 647–652.

Molleson, T. I. (1986). Skeletal age and paleodemography. In A. H. B. A. K. J. Collins (Ed.), *The Biology of Human Ageing*. Cambridge: Cambridge University Press.

Ortner, D. J. (2002). *Identification of Pathological Conditions in Human Skeletal Remains* (2nd ed.). Academic Press.

Pokines, J. T., & Symes, S. A. (2014). *Manual of forensic taphonomy*. Boca Raton [Fla.]: Taylor & Francis.

Redfield, A. (1970). A new aid to aging immature skeletons: development of the occipital bone. *American Journal of Physical Anthropology*, *33*(2), 207. Retrieved from http://murdoch.summon.serialssolutions.com/2.0.0/link/0/eLvHCXMwtV1bS8MwFA7TIYgg3oZ38j462jS9RPBhyMZ81e15pLnAkLUD9-K_9yRp2joQ9cGXUBIINN_pyTnpyfchFJNRGOz4BJFwDeZMOE1kKHLJVMR1lORcqzhLUu3ZGWyZaq_nz992Slf_C3joA-jNRdo_gN9MCh3wDCYALRgBtL8yg7HRDB_ylTRBplMkWq3Xls1z-P4Gew7EfrYqTrbVQ75uoBJiZUVFhkVVfikZav7zdIgnNh5x3movNOf1L0o2Ytjj9qQhYka-QhvmThtZ7MuqEZ0bKOUxIgYI8dRyO3qM6aovackjXPTqF2866b9Z24aklBiM_Du5wY_sRQ5O-liuxfVRlsHjdQ31z48j46cnztNmYIbZLfTZkXuMQHdQT7OQUNraYnYn6DjOinAYwffKeqp8gwddTQsPs7RbIwBSQxI4m2FLZLYI4kbJB9wB0dcaQw44g-ZHbHC8QIvpZP40C2oZjEBA-p0GVMHmKHVOeBHxTEguOc3ShMQiYrSAgBtSDpqFsFGAM44EV3GcykISwahKOZNkgPZLmP4SYZ2IiCrBdaiNxgotGKOaCA55rQ-ppJK_QwK3DcuO4Tpb1All_N3CDDltTuUV9Dd-NumvEuO4tAp_SjUL2.

Rocchi, A., Presciuttini, S., Chiti, E., Pierotti, S., & Spinetti, I. (2019). Identification of an exhumed corpse by DNA extraction from bulb swab. A disputed parentage case report. *Science & Justice*, *59*(2), 214–216. Available from https://doi.org/10.1016/j.scijus.2018.10.001.

Scheuer, L., & Black, S. (2000). *Developmental Juvenile Osteology*. Elsevier Ltd.

Scheuer, L., & MacLaughlin-Black, S. (1994). Age estimation from the pars basilaris of the fetal and juvenile occipital bone. *International Journal of Osteoarchaeology*, *4* (4), 377–380. Available from https://doi.org/10.1002/oa.1390040412.

Sledzik, P. S., & Willcox, A. W. (2009). Corpi aquaticus - The Hardin Cemetery Flood of 1993. In D. W. Steadman (Ed.), *Hard evidence: case studies in forensic anthropology* (2nd edition ed., p. 336). New Jersey - U.S.A: Prentice Hall.

Stray, J. E., & Shewale, J. G. (2010). Extraction of DNA from human remains. *Forensic Science Review*, *22*(2), 177–185.

Ubelaker, D. H. (1978). *Human skeletal remains: excavation, analysis, interpretation*. Washington, DC: Smithsonian Institute Press.

Ubelaker, D. H. (2014). Osteology reference collections. In C. Smith (Ed.), *Encyclopedia of global archaeology* (pp. 5632–5641). New York, NY: Springer New York.

van den Berge, M., Wiskerke, D., Gerretsen, R. R. R., Tabak, J., & Sijen, T. (2016). DNA and RNA profiling of excavated human remains with varying postmortem intervals. *International Journal of Legal Medicine*, *130*(6), 1471–1480. Available from https://doi.org/10.1007/s00414-016-1438-9.

Waldron, T. (2009). *Palaeopathology* (illustrat ed.). Cambridge; New York: Cambridge University Press.

Zvelebil, M., & Weber, A. W. (2013). Human bioarchaeology: Group identity and individual life histories – Introduction. *Journal of Anthropological Archaeology*, *32*(3), 275–279. Available from https://doi.org/10.1016/j.jaa.2012.01.003.

CHAPTER 6

A missing grandmother and a near-miss for justice

Edda Emanuela Guareschi
Medical, Molecular and Forensic Sciences, College of Science, Health, Engineering and Education, Murdoch University, Murdoch, WA, Australia

ABSTRACT
A cold case was reopened three years later, following a suspect's confession. The victim, a mature lady suffering from Alzheimer's disease, was murdered for financial reasons, and her body was dumped in the backyard of an abandoned country house. She was positively identified by genetic analysis on her skeletal remains. The inexperience of the expert witness appointed by the procurator led to the necessity of a reassessment of the skeletal remains, in order to perform a thorough bone trauma analysis, which unearthed a history of domestic violence and abuse dating back at least several years before the homicide. Bone trauma analysis is crucial in the examination of skeletal remains, and it must be distinguished from both pathology and taphonomy. Once established, it should be investigated with regards to antemortem, perimortem or postmortem changes. The case showed a lack of understanding by the Italian judicial system and highlighted the significance of the cooperation between forensic pathologists and forensic anthropologists in the study of skeletal remains.

Keywords: Forensic anthropology; domestic abuse; bone trauma analysis; taphonomy; heterotopic ossification

The intricacy of the diverse disciplinary and procedural levels of this forensic case, besides being a cold one, made it a unique and unforgettable experience in my career. The combination of a perplexed prosecutor, a worried defence attorney, superficial, unofficial and inexperienced expert witnesses and two defendants of the same family, embodies the perfect terrain for one or more professional faults and social faux-pas, as well as the objective difficulty of solving a cold case.

Forensic Pathology Case Studies. DOI: https://doi.org/10.1016/B978-0-12-824294-0.00009-1

In July 2012, a 63 years old lady suffering from Alzheimer's disease at an early stage was reported missing from her home. She lived as part of a large intergenerational family—her mother in her late eighties, a middle-aged daughter and four teenage grandchildren. Law enforcement apparently searched for her in the course of the following few weeks, but after a lack of further leads in the case, they dismissed it, filed it under voluntary disappearance, and with time it just went cold. More than three years later, in November 2015, one of the victim's grandchildren was overcome by guilt and confessed the homicide. Teaming up with his mother, who was the deceased's middle-aged daughter and principal caregiver, and under her influence and suggestion, he assisted in the asphyxiation of his grandmother for financial reasons. The deceased was sedated by drugs, and then a plastic bag was wrapped around her head and secured at her neck with twine, thus preventing her breathing. The young man, although not an adult at the time of the homicide but an adult at the time of the confession, led the police to the place where his grandmother's body had been dumped, the bushy backyard of a long-time abandoned and decrepit country house. The house was located 450 km away from the town where the family still lived, and where the victim had been initially reported missing. The victim's skeletal remains were positively identified by genetic analysis.

Up until this point, the case might have seemed routine, however, the complication started with the appointment of an inhospitable expert witness. The forensic pathologist, like many forensic pathologists, had no training in forensic anthropology. Instead of discussing the issue with the prosecutor, and demanding the official designation of a forensic anthropology expert witness to cooperate in the case, the anthropological analysis was managed by an inexperienced young graduated. The outcome of this cooperation was a meagre and unclear court report, which did not shed any light, let alone resolve, any aspect of the criminal event. While the report stalled with the prosecutor, the defendant's attorney started to worry and appointed a forensic pathology and anthropology expert witness, as it is allowed by the Italian law. I was requested to examine the skeletal remains and express my professional opinion about the cause, mode and manner of death of the victim. While I still was at the planning stage of this task, the two defendants, who were on trial, were accusing each other about the murder specifics, and their depositions revealed a history of domestic violence and abuse dating back at least several years. As a consequence, my task proved more difficult than expected, because beyond the aim of clarifying the circumstances of death, a thorough bone trauma analysis became even more imperative. The analysis would help establish both the extent and the timeline of the abuse, and consequently the truthfulness of the defendants' testimony.

From a strict forensic pathology perspective, the absence of the hyoid bone among the skeletal remains did not rule out of mechanical asphyxia as the cause of death, for example strangulation. Turning to the forensic anthropology investigation, after having assessed that several skeletal elements were missing and several ribs were fragmented, the first major differentiation required was between pathology and trauma/taphonomy. The second essential examination concerned the timing of bone trauma, by determining when it occurred, antemortem, perimortem or postmortem. Overall, the abuse evident on the victim was confirmed as having occurred between a few weeks and possibly more than one year before death. Several fractures were observed in different stages of remodelling, specifically of the right zygomatic bone (Fig. 6.1), the II left rib (Fig. 6.2), the right radial head (Fig. 6.3) and the vertebral column (multifocal) (Figs. 6.4–6.6). A fracture of the occipital bone, produced with mixed characteristics between blunt and sharp force, was inflicted perimortem with a shovel, in a botched attempt to dismember the body a few hours after death (Fig. 6.7). Another eight small and superficial fractures, sometimes called "hairline", were also produced on the cranial vault by the pointed tip of the same shovel. Three ribs were also fractured, but they lacked any clear antemortem or

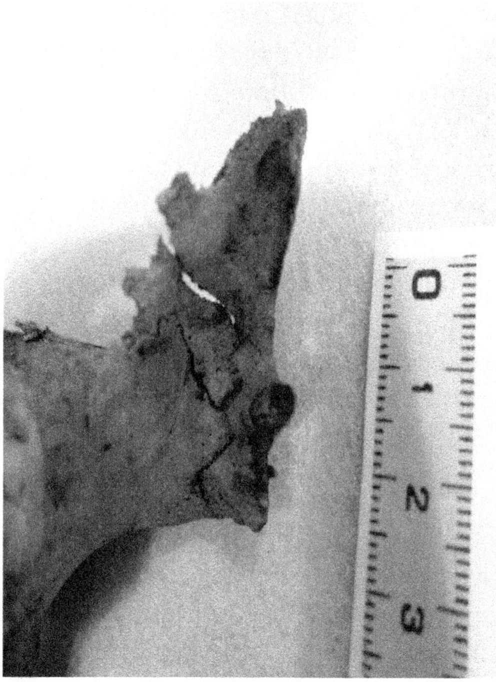

Figure 6.1 Fracture of the right zygomatic bone.

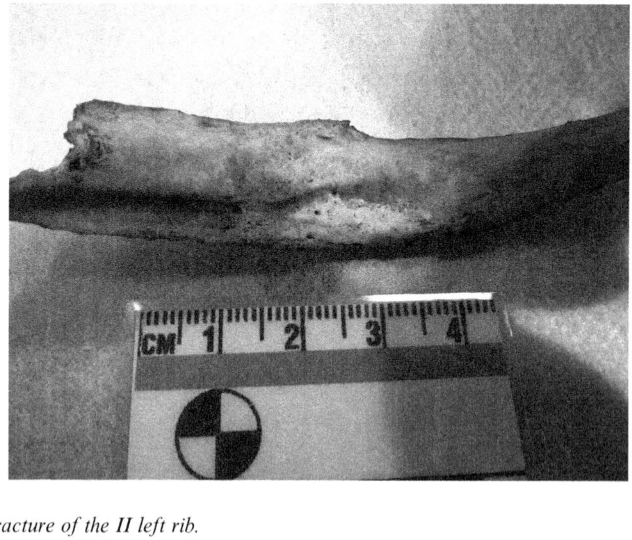

Figure 6.2 Fracture of the II left rib.

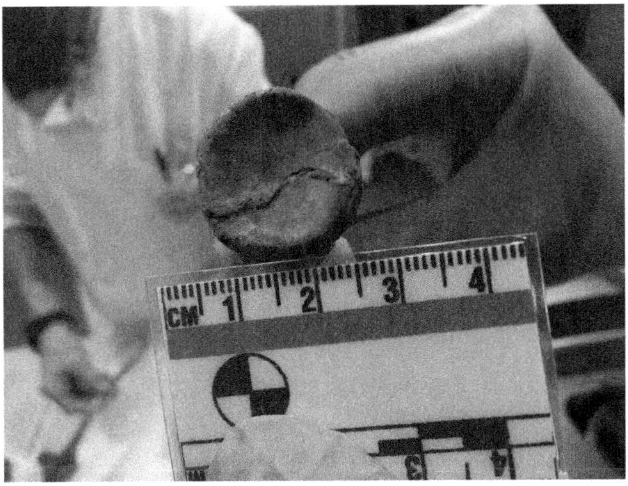

Figure 6.3 Fracture of the right radial head.

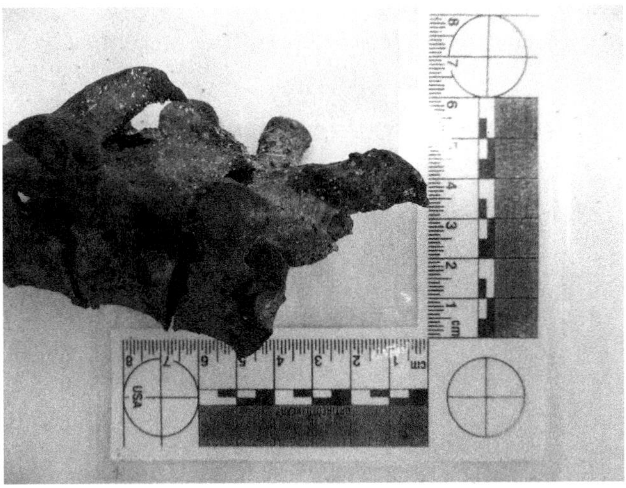

Figure 6.4 Fracture of the spinous process of D5.

obvious postmortem aspects, and they were assigned to the perimortem time range (Fig. 6.8).

The perimortem fractures of the three left ribs might have been produced in the time interval of a few hours around death, when the victim might have fallen due to sedative drugs, which she was unknowingly administered or when the body came to its

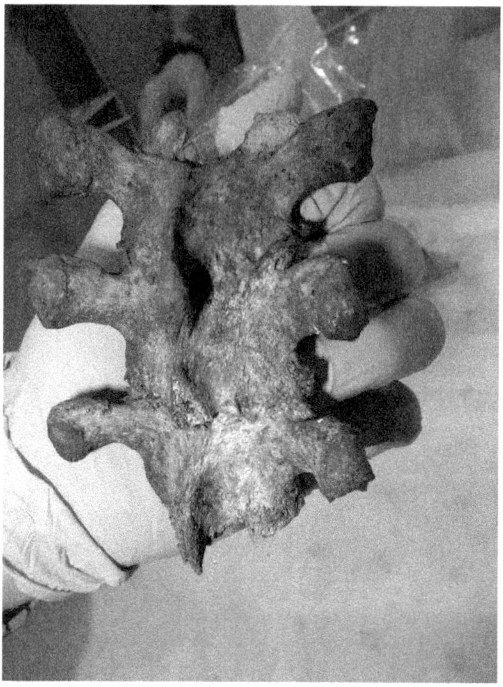

Figure 6.5 Heterotopic ossification of the posterior spinal ligaments in D3-D4-D5.

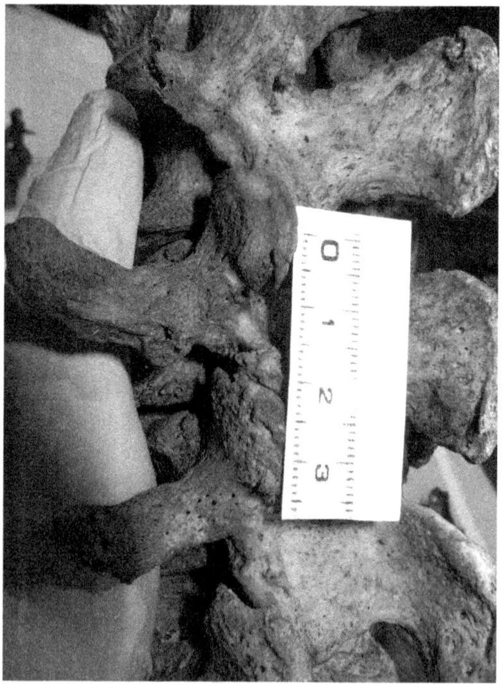

Figure 6.6 Fracture of the left transverse process of L3.

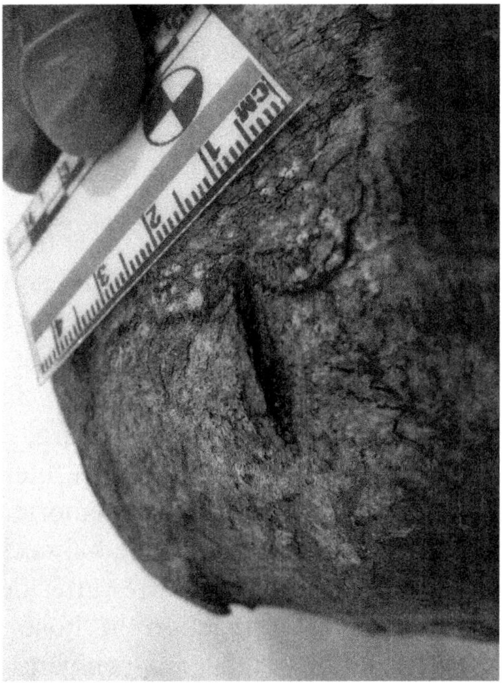

Figure 6.7 Fracture of the occipital bone.

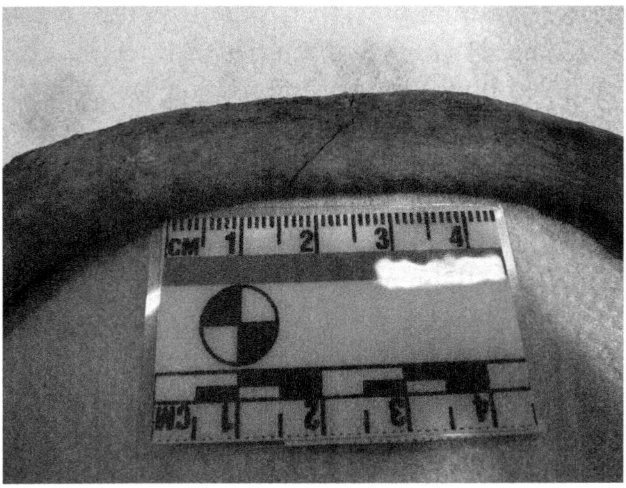

Figure 6.8 Fracture of a left rib.

ultimate location by being dumped off a flight of stairs into an overgrown backyard, where it was recovered. Finally, the diffuse erosion of cortical bone, with exposure of the inner trabecular architecture, typified features consistent with postmortem taphonomic damage. Bone trauma analysis is outlined in Table 6.1.

Once pathology and traumatic/taphonomic findings are differentiated, the next crucial distinction in similar cases of completely skeletonized remains encompasses the distinction between taphonomy and trauma and the timing of trauma (de Gruchy & Rogers, 2002; Houck, 1998; Passalacqua & Rainwater, 2015; Pokines & Symes, 2014; Sorg, 2019; Ubelaker & Adams, 1995). According to the extensive literature on bone trauma analysis, the characteristics of antemortem, perimortem and postmortem trauma are related to the biomechanical plasticity of bone (which progressively decreases after death), the presence- or absence- of a vital reaction in bone and/or in the surrounding soft tissues, and the environment of deposition/recovery of the body (Maples, 1998; Sauer, 1998). Obvious antemortem injuries present traces of the biological reaction of any living tissue to the loss of integrity, that is a trend to healing, portrayed by inflammation (periostitis), callus formation and bone remodelling. Postmortem injuries show physical alterations, globally included under the taphonomy umbrella, attributable to natural elements (Quatrehomme & İşcan, 1997), animal (Haglund, Reay, & Swindler, 1988) or human action (Bohnert, Rost, Faller-Marquardt, Ropohl, & Pollak, 1997; Mann & Owsley, 1992; Reichs, 1998), with respective examples like weathering cracks (Behrensmeyer, 1978), teeth marks from scavenging and lighter discolouring of margins of fractures produced during rough excavations. Perimortem injuries are the most difficult to assess (Cappella et al., 2014; Pechníková, Porta, & Cattaneo, 2011), since they were apparently produced in an undefined time interval around the time of death, when soft tissues are still present and the elasticity of bone is unaltered, but the healing process does not occur. The presence of a vital reaction of bone in perimortem injuries, as well as the beginning of

Table 6.1 Bone trauma analysis.

Type of lesion and anatomical location	Antemortem characteristics	Perimortem characteristics	Postmortem characteristics
Eight fractures on the cranial vault		– Tiny and superficial – absence of vital and/or taphonomic signs	
Fracture of the occipital bone		– Irregular, crushed and sharp margins – the walls of the fracture groove formed a right angle ("U"-shape) with the bottom – the bottom of the wound was rough – absence of vital and/or taphonomic signs	
Fracture of the right zygomatic bone	– Several ingrained fragments – bone remodelling		
Fracture of the II left rib	– Abundant bone callus – stable and evident bone remodelling		
Fractures of three left ribs		– Crushed margins with slight plastic deformation – absence of discoloration – absence of vital and/or taphonomic signs	
Fracture of the head of the right radius	– Advanced bone remodelling		
Heterotopic ossification of the posterior spinal ligaments ((Waldron, 2009)) (yellow, interspinous and capsular) at D3-D4-D5 level	– Complete heterotopic ossification, usually post-traumatic		
Spinous process of D5	– Periostitis		
Transverse process of L3	– Advanced bone remodelling		
Diffuse cortical bone			Erosion and exposure of the inner trabecular bone architecture

the healing process, have been recently examined through histology and immunohistochemistry on bone margins, and both techniques seem to be promising tools for further research on the matter (Cappella & Cattaneo, 2019; de Boer, van der Merwe, Hammer, Steyn, & Maat, 2015; Madea, Saukko, Oliva, & Musshoff, 2010).

Finally, this forensic case highlights a major flaw in the Italian judicial system. The so called well-defined and accepted rules concerning the requirements of specialized education and scientific reliability of expert witnesses are clearly inadequate. This might be supporting an arbitrary customary practice in appointments. Moreover, the significance of the cooperation between forensic pathologists and forensic anthropologists in the study of skeletal remains is once again highlighted. The correct assessment of the timing of injuries on bone might provide crucial information in any case history, with appropriate legal consequences. Citing this case as an example of a homicide which was preceded by years of abuse, the physical evidence of the abuse and an estimated timeline were paramount in the reconstruction of human behaviour, thus verifying the suspects' testimony.

References

Behrensmeyer, A. K. (1978). Taphonomic and ecologic information from bone weathering. *Paleobiology*, *4*(2), 150–162.

Bohnert, M., Rost, T., Faller-Marquardt, M., Ropohl, D., & Pollak, S. (1997). Fractures of the base of the skull in charred bodies — post-mortem heat injuries or signs of mechanical traumatisation? *Forensic Science International*, *87*(1), 55–62. Available from https://doi.org/10.1016/S0379-0738(97)02136-1.

Cappella, A., Amadasi, A., Castoldi, E., Mazzarelli, D., Gaudio, D., & Cattaneo, C. (2014). The difficult task of assessing perimortem and postmortem fractures on the skeleton: a blind text on 210 fractures of known origin. *Journal of Forensic Sciences*, *59*(6), 1598–1601. Available from https://doi.org/10.1111/1556-4029.12539.

Cappella, A., & Cattaneo, C. (2019). Exiting the limbo of perimortem trauma: a brief review of microscopic markers of hemorrhaging and early healing signs in bone. *Forensic Science International*, *302*, 109856. Available from https://doi.org/10.1016/j.forsciint.2019.06.014.

de Boer, H. H., van der Merwe, A. E., Hammer, S., Steyn, M., & Maat, G. J. R. (2015). Assessing post-traumatic time interval in human dry bone. *International*

Journal of Osteoarchaeology, *25*(1), 98–109. Available from https://doi.org/10.1002/oa.2267.

de Gruchy, S., & Rogers, T. L. (2002). Identifying chop marks on cremated bone: a preliminary study. *Journal of Forensic Sciences*, *47*(5), 933. Retrieved from http://murdoch.summon.serialssolutions.com/2.0.0/link/0/eLvHCXMwtV1LS8QwEA7qXgQR32_JfenSJH2KHkRc9Oqu5yVNUhHdblm87L93Jkm7ZUXRg5fSbSBL55tOJu183xAi-CAMVmJChHSQjKFUijJFKE0Zo9BWVqRFqVPbHWhZprpsPrpSuvpfwMM1gB6Jt-H8Av50ULsA5uAAcwQng-Cs3cERcR2aCSFf3p3L-Zj8RQLoI2SomoLPKOM5zPTfvtsvXfNHRnf2aukKii3Xvqu_XzzYv1-Bz4CwOuVGNY23x79Psxfdjg_VRLTzdoXnhwNuKqi4BgDHXPHpgfNyME9yK5t3A6qQ0vQPFnSiZO-2LjvnrqbU_EndF7BrC_Dy66IpLdDqFg-lS_qo8bUwXPo3XSQ-4RRuz7x2G7RCcsYY2MPN4JSsf6GVa2FzbNGO-QbW9keuuQ3CVrptojW-7lKnWcsX1y3UGVIqrUokpnFW1QpYjqFZW0gym1mB6Q8fB-fPcQ-DYYQZ1xFmghC5UppXUUqlQlWJlrUqOF4qZQAvJRGYc6ZEbIMhQi1kpgJRBs5SP4FQt-SDYq-MtjQjmTHBY4XagojfJS56koBVeRZFkOM2Qn5Mjd-6R2UieTxiqn346ckc2lk5yTXgkPjrlou3FdWsN_AhQAQEM.

Haglund, W. D., Reay, D. T., & Swindler, D. R. (1988). Tooth mark artifacts and survival of bones in animal scavenged human skeletons. *Journal of Forensic Sciences*, *33*(4), 985. Retrieved from http://murdoch.summon.serialssolutions.com/2.0.0/link/0/eLvHCXMwtV1LS8NAEF6qRSiI-Cq-2XtJySabNDl4EGnRi4c-8Fg2-yihNi196N93NpsXEVEPXkLZhZDsN539djLzDUKu07Wtmk8gwnGVLrqG_ZBLqhxOA8ZlRIHt-KkfYuTpDmqbaaOQf02upq_8FPIwB9LqQ9g_gFzeFAfgNJgBXMAK4_s4MlgBFZ8-HWcy1nFOs6BqPKvNmBk3g3VDTSgv068sGSeJFWSeom8zPgoqaF32YOm9M2D-x9pbJAfHUePO9k--mm9Guzt50JXb-WucVDycy3-zJDe_QRa7WHtRkelrEIEsJS53mr1doAQkxf6a7MXKrn61NqWPW5Rvwisy1acaChaeBTQWa1SKEBngPkhPw4WVPPz-me0kPpCxHx7LxNrMtpDTV2TpD15_3lQbN0-8UkuL69fo4UOshvUTh0p-xgfo6NsrfGDAfgENWRyig5NzBWbUrIz9JKCjTXYuAAbA9g4BxsvFU7BxnGCDdi4ABunY-OMC7HM0GfTHj09W1i_DYiToOZanaBRwFgIjY4I5bigUpVLRIOQ-sBDWY56K4HgLJwLpq0h6wE6lHxAuqB9Jypw22k_gGS4Q9sDBeD3BQ1syGkoWKDdwXcpEY-DuiF8lL1DbLMV0ZUZRptk5X301co1ZpMTeoqeAPJm-Lrl13KRCff7tQNg.

Houck, M. (1998). Skeletal trauma and the individualisation of knife marks in bone. In K. J. Reichs (Ed.), *Forensic osteology: advances in the identification of human remains*. Springfield: Charles C. Thomas Publisher.

Madea, B., Saukko, P., Oliva, A., & Musshoff, F. (2010). Molecular pathology in forensic medicine—Introduction. *Forensic Science International*, *203*(1), 3–14. Available from https://doi.org/10.1016/j.forsciint.2010.07.017.

Mann, R. W., & Owsley, D. W. (1992). Human osteology: key to the sequence of events in a postmortem shooting. *Journal of Forensic Sciences*, *37*(5), 1386. Retrieved from http://murdoch.summon.serialssolutions.com/2.0.0/link/0/eLvHCXMwtV3dS8MwEA_qEAYifg2_yXvpaJo23QQfhm7qk6Db80iyBPewduDAf99Lk7SlouiDL6UkNND73V3ujvtAiMb9KGzpBKYUZYkQaaYHgmiusqGW9v6WLCojGXWaaj18s5W6-l_AwxpAbwpp_wB-dSgswDuwADyBCeD5KzZwwycAS1uWQkcBiK23OH0itTEZy1ZOZXYsD9bwwapMww3e34pi4--3r1Ys2LwmBV4G7iqtTHQ_ffklqKI4zx8-Qn7vFheu_i6u8qma6f-E2NHRfeW0ZsqMIzpsqlXby8WxT9rQkYTa5tcN6q9XJfnB2Yudcv5xs9Uh2–YZumrxVJublUezl63UcfUHRltPX6aVNczI4z4FvLmP7po1x3Q8ixKC2N6gPYdUfH-YZumrxVJublUezl63UcfUHRltPX6aVNczI4z4FvLmP7po1x3Q8ixKC2N6gPYdUfHIgniItlR-hPZsXBXbcrFj9FACiitAbzDAiTcFBjixhxMXGls48TLHHNdwYg_nCZpNxtO7x9ANwwg5WFlJSBfgqKdcxEyBmUq50BycTZJx8A-51FpERIpISJJFiiaSDXWkRCyyGAQsGVAZ99BOXuTqFGEQRpVGXBJKVZKKRKg4k5GZi7DQ4OHSM9Sz-dJivbceTuSPQ-XcbF6hb88ol6miQHnVVjeS6LhH4BCaFQpk.

Maples, M. R. (1998). Trauma analysis by the forensic anthropologist. In K. J. Reichs (Ed.), *Forensic osteology: advances in the identification of human remains*. Springfield: Charles C. Thomas Publisher.

Passalacqua, N. V. E., & Rainwater, C. W. E. (2015). *Skeletal trauma analysis*. Chichester, West Sussex: Wiley Blackwell.

Pechníková, M., Porta, D., & Cattaneo, C. (2011). Distinguishing between perimortem and postmortem fractures: are osteons of any help? *International Journal of Legal Medicine*, *125*(4), 591–595. Available from https://doi.org/10.1007/s00414-011-0570-9.

Pokines, J. T., & Symes, S. A. (2014). *Manual of forensic taphonomy*. Boca Raton [Fla.]: Taylor & Francis.

Quatrehomme, G., & İşcan, M. Y. (1997). Postmortem skeletal lesions. *Forensic Science International*, *89*(3), 155–165. Available from https://doi.org/10.1016/S0379-0738(97)00113-8.

Reichs, K. J. (1998). Postmortem dismemberment: recovery, analysis and interpretation. In K. J. Reichs (Ed.), *Forensic Osteology: advances in the identification of human remains*. Springfield: Charles C. Thomas Publisher.

Sauer, N. (1998). The timing of injuries and manner of death: distinguishing among antemortem, perimortem and postmortem trauma. In K. J. Reichs (Ed.), *Forensic Osteology: advances in the identification of human remains*. Springfield: Charles C. Thomas Publisher.

Sorg, M. H. (2019). Differentiating trauma from taphonomic alterations. *Forensic Science International*, *302*, 109893. Available from https://doi.org/10.1016/j.forsciint.2019.109893.

Ubelaker, D. H., & Adams, B. J. (1995). Differentiation of perimortem and postmortem trauma using taphonomic indicators. *Journal of Forensic Sciences*, *40*(3), 509. Retrieved from http://murdoch.summon.serialssolutions.com/2.0.0/link/0/eLvHCXMwtV1La8JAEF5spSCU0pf0zd4l4ibuxhx6sFVpTz1Uz7LZBxRqlBr_f2cfeRCwtIdegmYh4n6zs99s5ptBKAr7g6DhE3gohiOqCRUJxBNSSfCYPGWcccGS0UAU1RlsmmqrVail-G6mr_wU83APojZD2D-CXD4Ub8BlMAK5gBHD9lRlMfAOU_KPkhrakv82xdVUC1tvcf82_-G7Fezt7fpBzk7ZuRMs9815bmOh8u4fLAvM1ifCi5zfUkqgvUvXJfeLGpBJCjKU_4nnyr6WkF-LRKsuvpgMgxPWQ7ivvPikzEWlS96-uHJO3o6jmLKktjJDXUNisLAwx0JbYtRn4cbBRKbsYMUXTVzAv-aPKgsX7AWob_ZHx2tPXWblNM8JIUUre_I0OOvIPaEQYlmnMT9GJn1Y8dmCeoZbKztGxO1_FTjZ2gd4awOK1xhWwGIDFFbDYAYstsLgCFlfAXqLFbDp_fgl8cwxYS-GQBrByBLBDRrkyKh9JqKQyYcDeGEl1AmtN0ERRIHx6yCMCtDImqQoV8GOI4akKu-gwW2fqCmEGQaPmNFVUAxvVcqRVNGQihN1AxfBj16jr5mO5cRVQln6ibvYN3KJOZTJ3qK1hNan7skXXg0XiG1vcSmQ.

Waldron, Tony (2009). Palaeopathology. Cambridge University Press.

SECTION 3

Casework of Forensic Imaging and Legal Medicine

CHAPTER 7

A complex case of neglect and mental disability

Edda Emanuela Guareschi[1], Maria Laura Schirripa[2] and Paola Annarosa Magni[1,3]

[1]Medical, Molecular and Forensic Sciences, College of Science, Health, Engineering and Education, Murdoch University, Murdoch, WA, Australia, [2]Dipartimento di Medicina e Chirurgia, Universita' di Parma, Parma, Italy, [3]Murdoch University Singapore, Singapore

ABSTRACT

In this case, a 43 years old mentally disabled man died of septic shock, caused by severe and untreated burns. He lived in an apartment in a flat complex, owned and also inhabited by his mother and various relatives who, beyond denying any knowledge of his living conditions, did not seek any medical assistance after a fire broke out into his apartment a few days before death. The carcasses of a dog, a cat and a turtle in different stages of decomposition were also found in the apartment. The following investigation, beyond cause, mode and manner of death, was directed to assess the timeline of the deceased's mental disability, thus the duration of potential neglect from the family part. The investigation was multidisciplinary, and it revealed about 20 years of neglect of a person whose mental disability was completely unknown by health, social and welfare services. The veterinary forensics assessment determined that also the pets were neglected, and most likely starved to death.

Keywords: Mental disability; adult neglect; elderly neglect; animal cruelty; veterinary forensics

After years of forensic pathology practice, even after reading case work, studying and visiting other institutions worldwide, some of which big and challenging, one should not be lulled into believing oneself psychologically ready for any future case. There are cases that can still defy one's understanding of human behaviour. On a late and cold Friday evening in February 2016, I was called to a death scene investigation in what had once been a village, but had by then become an outer city residential suburb. A 43 years old man was found dead in his apartment,

Forensic Pathology Case Studies. DOI: https://doi.org/10.1016/B978-0-12-824294-0.00002-9

located in a small flat complex owned and inhabited by his parents and other relatives. Together with a young trainee, I drove to the place expecting a mundane case, as if it is ever possible to apply mundane to a forensic pathologist's routine, but we were completely unprepared for what we were about to see.

Law enforcement officers were already inside the apartment, the door was ajar and the first thing that struck us when we glimpsed through the door opening was a very dark crime scene. This was due to the absence of any light bulbs and the complete closure of the window shutters. From the bedroom, located at the end of a short entrance corridor, came a dim light. Holding a flashlight, we made our way through the corridor, wading through ankle deep garbage, and as we proceeded, we noticed that the access to all other rooms in the house was prevented by higher piles of garbage and stacked furniture (Figs. 7.1 and 7.2).

What had once been the kitchen and the bathroom were almost unreachable, and of course unserviceable, due to cobwebs, garbage and dirt. During our advance to the bedroom some garbage was displaced, revealing the carcasses of a dog, a cat and a turtle in different stages of decomposition (Fig. 7.3).

In the bedroom the bed quilt and the curtains were partially burnt, and a body lay on the floor. The deceased was naked, cachectic and covered in dirt. The left side of the face and the trunk, the left arm and the left thigh presented infected burns in all stages of classification, from the first-degree to the fourth-degree levels of severity.

The examinations of the body started the following Monday, and a multidisciplinary expertise was required to assess the cause, mode and manner of death. The prosecutor, in fact, deemed it necessary to complete the investigation by estimating the time of death and the amount of time during which the victim had lived in that apartment in such dire conditions. A 2D full-body CT scan was performed to exclude the presence of further lesions, in

Figure 7.1 The entrance corridor.

comparison to those observed during the death scene investigation, and to obtain a guide for the following external examination and autopsy workflow. The CT scan revealed a massive loss of tissue in the anterior left thoracic wall and in the left forearm. In the oral cavity, a 3D scan reconstruction detected multiple periapical granulomas in both dental arcades, a fistula into the right maxillary sinus, a palatal cyst with involvement of the cortical bone in the dental element 21, a restoration in 26, root fragments in 37 and 38, an avulsion in 41, lesion of furcation in 46 and 47 and a serious and widespread parodontopathy. The external examination of the body confirmed very poor personal hygiene, low body weight with diffused muscle hypotrophy and first- to fourth-degree burns in a large area in the upper left body, with

Figure 7.2 The light from bedroom, in the background on the right.

focal tissue necrosis and an exposed bone in the left wrist. The autopsy revealed cerebral and pulmonary oedema and mild arteriosclerosis; the cause of death was determined to be septic shock following untreated, extended and infected burns. The victim died several days after the occurrence of the burns, caused by a fire that broke out in his bedroom, most likely on account of an unextinguished cigarette stub. The manner of death was consequently classified as accidental.

Further ancillary investigations were conducted in the disciplines of anthropology, entomology, toxicology and veterinary forensics. The observation by stereomicroscopy of the exposed distal end of the left ulna ruled out any signs of animal activity,

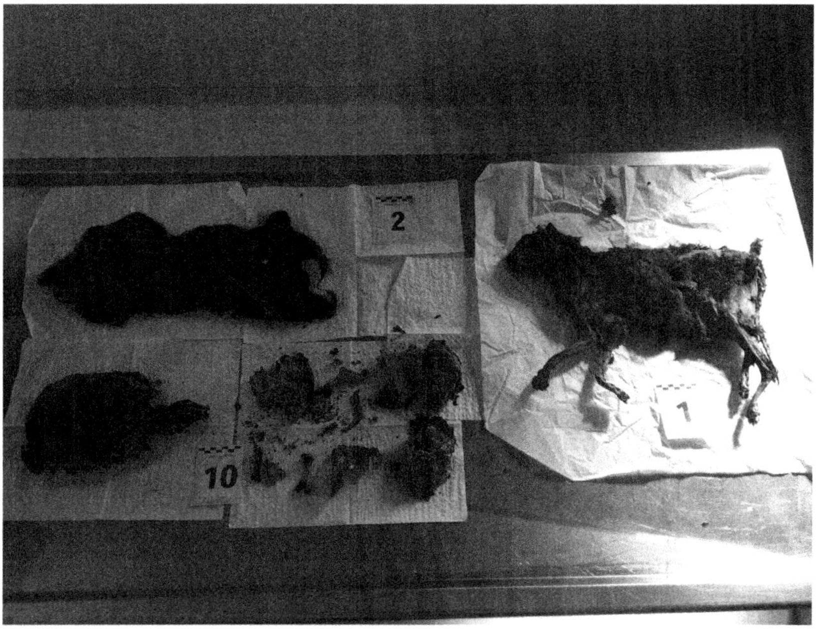

Figure 7.3 Carcasses of a dog, a cat and a turtle.

including the gnawing of small rodents, which was initially suspected. The exposition of the bone was ascribed to the necrosis of the overlying skin, following the burn. The toxicological analyses detected benzodiazepines and paracetamol in concentrations consistent with therapeutic ranges.

The entomological analysis considered only the remains of the immature insects collected during the death scene investigation. No living insects—either immature or adult—were observed in the apartment. The large number of empty pupal cases of flies (Diptera: Calliphoridae) was associated with the extensive colonisations of the carcasses of the pets, active in the previous months or year. The entomological assessment was consistent with the veterinary forensics findings, agreeing that the estimated time since death of the pets was at least one year before the death of their owner. Since no trauma was detected on the carcasses, the cause of death of the pets was presumed to be a combination of neglect and starvation. The absence of any living insects on the human body was consistent with the estimation of the time since death, just a few hours before recovery.

The prosecutor's question concerning the deceased's way of life was twofold as to whether the deceased had deliberately chosen it or if neglect was involved. Neglect is a criminal act directed at adults, such as parents or guardians of children, who should provide them with nutrition and proper care (Logan-Greene & Semanchin Jones, 2015; Saukko & Knight, 2016; Wen et al., 2019). Adults with physical or mental disabilities can also be victims of neglect (Hughes et al., 2012). The police investigation on this case lasted some considerable time after I submitted my pathology report, and several circumstantial details of the case were the topic of many conversations I had with the prosecutor. The deceased was a schizophrenic who had not been able to care for himself for about 20 years. In spite of this, he had always refused any psychiatric assessment, he was unknown by social services and his General Practitioner had not seen him for more than 10 years. His mother, who lived in another apartment in the same building, provided him food sustenance and, from time to time, some mild anxiolytic drugs prescribed in her name. The other relatives, also living in different apartments in the same building, denied all knowledge about the situation. When a fire broke out in the deceased's bedroom, a few days before his death, no one came to his assistance. The poor man had simply been abandoned, relegated to the margins of the society and deprived of access to treatment by his own family. On that basis, the case was defined as neglect of a mentally disabled person, and every adult member of the family was charged.

The definition of neglect as ascribed by the WHO in 1999 is "child abuse or maltreatment constitutes all forms of physical and/or emotional ill-treatment, sexual abuse, neglect or negligent treatment or commercial or other exploitation, resulting in actual or potential harm to the child's health, survival, development or dignity in the context of a relationship of responsibility, trust or power." (Krug, Dahlberg, Mercy, Zwi, & Lozano, 2002).

In particular, neglect refers to the failure of a parent or a guardian to provide for the development of the child's health, education, emotional development, nutrition, shelter and safe living conditions. Abuse and neglect do not only concern children, but also refers to the so-called "vulnerable" subjects, such as the elderly and/or physically or psychologically ill people (Keywood, 2017; Storey & Prashad, 2018; Ventura, Caputo, & Molinelli, 2018). Cases similar to this raise a critical question about such a dramatic social problem: how is it possible to assess the mental disability of an uncooperative adult (Linden, 2017)? How many similar cases do exist, hidden within the walls of ordinary houses, lived in by apparently normal families?

Finally, the neglected pets should not be forgotten, since they were the other silent victims in this sad story. To date, cruelty to animals has been recognised as a felony in most industrialized and many developing countries (https://www.animalsandsociety.org/resources/animal-protection-laws-by-country/), and as a consequence this should duly lead to the worldwide academic, financial and professional endorsement of veterinary forensics, a rising discipline during the last decade (Brundage & Byrd, 2016; Merck, 2013; Parry & Stoll, 2020).

References

Brundage, A., & Byrd, J. H. (2016). Forensic entomology in animal cruelty cases. *Veterinary Pathology*, *53*(5), 898–909. Available from https://doi.org/10.1177/0300985816651683.

Hughes, K., Bellis, M. A., Jones, L., Wood, S., Bates, G., Eckley, L., … Officer, A. (2012). Prevalence and risk of violence against adults with disabilities: a systematic review and meta-analysis of observational studies. *The Lancet (British edition)*, *379* (9826), 1621–1629. Available from https://doi.org/10.1016/S0140-6736(11)61851-5.

Keywood, K. (2017). The vulnerable adult experiment: Situating vulnerability in adult safeguarding law and policy. *International Journal of Law and Psychiatry*, *53*, 88–96. Available from https://doi.org/10.1016/j.ijlp.2017.05.011.

Krug, E. G., Dahlberg, L. L., Mercy, J. A., Zwi, A. B., & Lozano, R. (2002). *World report on violence and health*. Geneva: World Health Organization.

Linden, M. (2017). Definition and assessment of disability in mental disorders under the perspective of the International Classification of Functioning Disability and Health (ICF). *Behavioral Sciences & the Law*, *35*(2), 124–134. Available from https://doi.org/10.1002/bsl.2283.

Logan-Greene, P., & Semanchin Jones, A. (2015). Chronic neglect and aggression/delinquency: A longitudinal examination. *Child Abuse & Neglect*, *45*, 9–20. Available from https://doi.org/10.1016/j.chiabu.2015.04.003.

Merck, M. (2013). *Veterinary forensics: animal cruelty investigations* (2nd ed.). Ames, Iowa: John Wiley & Sons, Inc.

Parry, N. M. A., & Stoll, A. (2020). The rise of veterinary forensics. *Forensic Science International*, *306*, 110069. Available from https://doi.org/10.1016/j.forsciint.2019.110069.

Saukko, P. J. A., & Knight, B. A. (2016). *Knight's forensic pathology* (Fourth ed.). Boca Raton: CRC Press.

Storey, J. E., & Prashad, A. A. (2018). Recognizing, reporting, and responding to abuse, neglect, and self-neglect of vulnerable adults: an evaluation of the react adult protection worker basic curriculum. *Journal of Elder Abuse & Neglect*, *30*(1), 42–63. Available from https://doi.org/10.1080/08946566.2017.1371092.

Ventura, F., Caputo, F., & Molinelli, A. (2018). Medico-legal aspects of deaths related to neglect and abandonment in the elderly. *Aging clinical and experimental research*, *30*(11), 1399–1402. Available from https://doi.org/10.1007/s40520-018-0912-2.

Wen, Y.-J., Li, X.-B., Zhao, X.-X., Wang, X.-Q., Hou, W.-P., Bo, Q.-J., … Wang, C.-Y. (2019). The effect of left-behind phenomenon and physical neglect on behavioral problems of children. *Child Abuse & Neglect*, *88*, 144–151. Available from https://doi.org/10.1016/j.chiabu.2018.11.007.

CHAPTER 8

Postmortem imaging in forensic cases

Edda Emanuela Guareschi

Medical, Molecular and Forensic Sciences, College of Science, Health, Engineering and Education, Murdoch University, Murdoch, WA, Australia

ABSTRACT

Postmortem imaging is the application to forensics of imaging techniques used in the routine assessment of clinical diagnoses. The techniques involve, but are not limited to, ultrasound, X-rays, computed tomography and magnetic resonance. The aim of postmortem imaging is to complement, and in some cases substitute, traditional autopsies. Postmortem imaging has developed dramatically since the turn of the millennium. In 2011, the International Society of Forensic Radiology and Imaging (ISFRI) was founded, and in 2013 the related journal was launched. An updated list of imaging techniques and a summary of five cases are outlined in this chapter. The findings in the case study vary from incidental to elements of personal identification, through imaging misdiagnosis and bone trauma analysis. Finally, postmortem imaging is almost always carried out before a traditional autopsy, but a post autopsy imaging is justified in limited cases.

Keywords: Postmortem imaging; Virtopsy; 3D printing; hyperostosis frontalis interna (HFI); post autopsy imaging

When I first approached forensic pathology, in the late 1990s, postmortem imaging was not mentioned in pathology courses at universities and did not appear in classical forensic pathology textbooks. In the forensic practice, it embodied a rarely addressed niche topic, and its applications were reserved to carefully selected cases, such as personal identification from skeletal remains by comparison of antemortem and postmortem X-rays of the paranasal cranial sinuses or dentition, the need to locate a foreign object in a body when an impractical anatomical location was suspected, or to assess age in the living. Even in those cases, the technique was limited to classical X-rays, and the

Forensic Pathology Case Studies. DOI: https://doi.org/10.1016/B978-0-12-824294-0.00003-0

process of obtaining a postmortem imaging examination was long and troublesome. In fact, the overwhelming majority of morgues did not possess any imaging equipment, so pathologists had to rely on the involvement of medical imaging hospital departments, ordinarily reserved to, and accessed by, high numbers of living patients. The noble purpose of serving justice ensured the cooperation of the imaging departments staff, but that cooperation was not achieved without resistances and veiled conflicts about various issues, summarized in the transport of bodies or skeletal remains, the time of the day in which they could be unloaded into the facility without drawing undesired attentions—this ended up at invariably awkward hours very early in the morning or late at night—the duration of the examination, usually performed by disgruntled staff working overtime, and the compliance to hygiene requirements.

By the turn of the millennium the technological development of imaging methods had become impressive, and the forensic pathology community had completely acknowledged their huge potential. At the same time, the reasonable lowering of costs allowed hospitals and institutions to increase their imaging equipment, and the additional use of postmortem imaging to traditional investigations, such as external examination and autopsy, timidly unfolded. The application of postmortem imaging to forensic pathology started as unorganized in institutions worldwide, but soon a proposal of harmonization and standard codification was launched through Virtopsy, a Swiss project characterized by a trans-disciplinary research approach to establish minimally invasive routine imaging methods to complement, or even substitute, traditional autopsies. The pillars of Virtopsy can be condensed in documentation methods (photogrammetry, 3D optical scanning, minimally invasive image-guided tissue sampling) and the achievement of a virtual autopsy by postmortem imaging, with critical advantages over a traditional autopsy, like the overall reduction of biohazard, the possibility of 2D and 3D image postprocessing and the creation of digital archives, easy to store and to retrieve at any time (Bolliger et al., 2007;

Thali, Jackowski, Oesterhelweg, Ross, & Dirnhofer, 2007). In 2011, the International Society of Forensic Radiology and Imaging (ISFRI) was founded with the aim of establishing scientific and operational standards in forensic and postmortem imaging; constant updates and periodic reviews have since been reported in the related journal since its inception, in January 2013 (Aalders et al., 2017; Baglivo et al., 2013; Carew & Errickson, 2019), with the newest frontier illustrated by 3D printing (Baier, Warnett, Payne, & Williams, 2018; Carew & Errickson, 2020; Ebert, Thali, & Ross, 2011).

Today, a postmortem imaging assessment by the technique/s believed to be the most appropriate before performing any other investigation, or between an external examination and a traditional autopsy, is highly recommended (Ahmad et al., 2017; Chatzaraki, Heimer, Thali, Dally, & Schweitzer, 2018; Cirielli et al., 2018; Flach et al., 2014; Jackowski et al., 2005; Tschui, Jackowski, Schwendener, Schyma, & Zech, 2016) and has become routine in most selected cases, including—but not limited to—the presence of foreign bodies enclosed in remains (Oesterhelweg, Bolliger, Thali, & Ross, 2009; Schweitzer et al., 2013; Thali et al., 2003; van Kan, Haest, Lahaye, & Hofman, 2017), postmortem changes (Christe et al., 2010; Franckenberg, Flach, Gascho, Thali, & Ross, 2015; Klein, Kunz, Hermans, Bayat, & Koopmanschap, 2016; Le Garff et al., 2017), trauma (Obertová et al., 2019), human pathology (Ampanozi et al., 2014; Charlier et al., 2011), veterinary forensics (Franckenberg, Kern, Vogt, Thali, & Flach, 2015), anthropology (Doyle et al., 2019; Simmons-Ehrhardt, Ehrhardt, & Monson, 2019; Tangmose, Jensen, & Lynnerup, 2013) and disaster victim identification (DVI) (Brough, Morgan, & Rutty, 2015; Iino & Aoki, 2016; Ruder et al., 2016). Depending on the case, the postmortem imaging assessment can either serve as a triage tool in the decisional process about the requirement of a subsequent traditional autopsy, or it can act as a complementing analysis.

The list of postmortem imaging techniques has dramatically expanded in the last ten years. The first distinction among imaging techniques is the modality of image acquisition, that is contact or non-contact, with regards to the object of investigation. Contact imaging techniques can be destructive, whereas non-contact techniques, which are never destructive, are distinguished in reflective, such as most surface scanning like photogrammetry, laser triangulation and structured light scanning, or transmissive, such as X-rays, computed tomography (CT) and magnetic resonance (MR). Postmortem CT (PMCT) and postmortem MR (PMMR) use is predominantly unenhanced, but intravascular media can be added to increase contrast in blood vessels. Enhanced PMCT and PMMR are known as PMCT angiography (PMCTA) and PMMR angiography (PMMRA). Sub-techniques of CT, like dual-energy CT and micro-CT, and ultrasound in the contact variant are reserved to selected cases. Some imaging techniques also work as guides to achieve needle biopsies of target organs. Finally, multimodal imaging combines data from multiple techniques. Technical considerations, protocols, advantages and limitations of different imaging techniques fall beyond the scope of this chapter, but can be found in the referenced literature.

In 2015, I involved two radiologists and three students in the collection of a few cases from the previous five years, 2010–2015, in which postmortem imaging had completed the forensic investigation. Once again, the aim of the collection was to enforce the vital role of postmortem imaging in selected forensic cases. However, it occurred to me that beyond findings with undoubtable and immediate forensic value, postmortem imaging techniques can also reveal unusual or incidental findings, that is any finding which purpose transcends forensic value, but adds relevant information to the case.

In Case 1, the naked body of a mature woman was found in a floodplain in the north of Italy. The flood had receded only a couple of days before the recovery of the body, however, an initial stage of adipocere was showing in subcutaneous tissues. A 2D full-body CT scan showed no trauma, but a small array of bone pathology, among which an increase of the thickness of the frontal bone, which could be interpreted either as a sign of

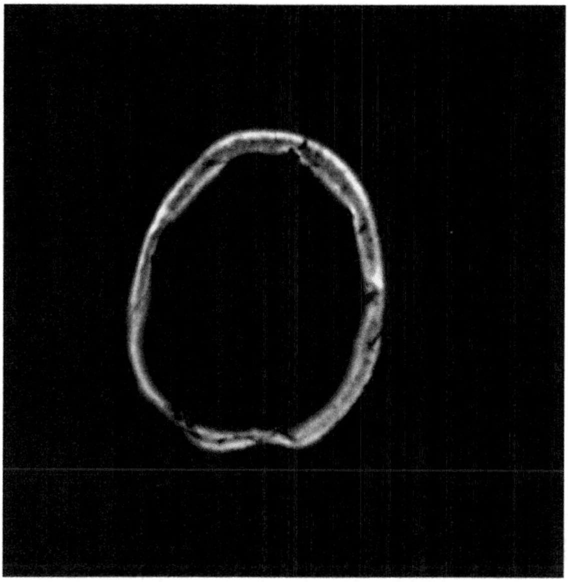

Figure 8.1 Hyperostosis frontalis interna.

several haematological, metabolic or infectious diseases, or as a benign process, surprisingly common in older women (Fig. 8.1). The benign condition is defined as hyperostosis frontalis interna (HFI), a precise aetiology is currently unknown, but suggestions have been expressed about a long-lasting exposure to oestrogen hormones. In specific literature, age is a significant predictor of HFI (Western & Bekvalac, 2017). Unfortunately, the poor woman was never identified and has been resting within an unmarked grave, in the local cemetery, for the last decade.

Case 2 portrayed the homicide of a 28 years old male sex worker. Before being finally killed by a stab wound in the abdomen, he had been violently beaten and strangled with a belt. A traditional X-ray of the head and the neck revealed a fracture of the left zygomatic bone (Fig. 8.2), which was added to the long list of perimortem trauma. That fracture might have been undetected at autopsy, especially if the external signs were ambiguous or mixed with other lesions. Furthermore, the anatomical area of the face is ordinarily undissected. To date, the case remains unsolved.

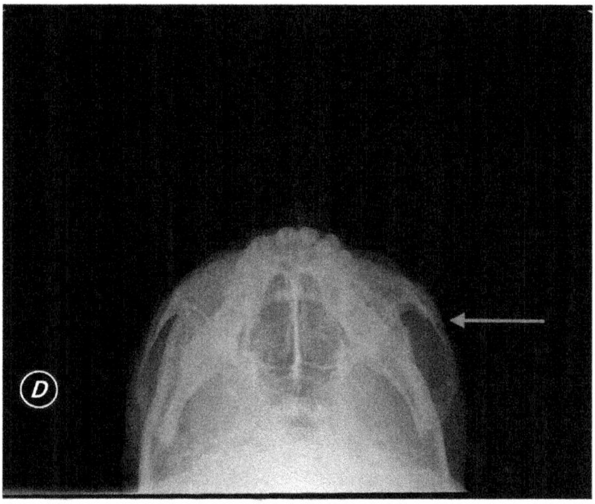

Figure 8.2 Fracture of the left zygomatic bone.

In Case 3, a 20 years old female sex worker was killed by ligature strangulation with a belt. The perpetrator was quickly apprehended, and at trial denied any beating of the victim. He declared that he had rendered the victim unconscious by manual strangulation and had used the belt of his trousers to ensure a fatal result. His version conflicted with a 2D CT scan to the head and neck of the victim, which was taken a couple of days after the recovery of the body and reported a fracture of the nasal bones. The fracture of the nasal bones could indicate a struggle, in which the victim attempted to fight, escape or defend herself. This could be used to evaluate the reliability of the perpetrator's statement. The CT scan was re-examined by two distinct observers, and they both agreed on the absence of any fracture (Fig. 8.3). Most likely, a combination of the inexperience of the first radiologist with postmortem imaging, and the young age of the victim, led to the mistaken interpretation of the nasofrontal and the frontomaxillary sutures as fractures.

At the death scene investigation of Case 4, in a cattleshed, the 46 years old milker was presumed accidentally killed by a kick from a cow he was milking. However, a traditional X-ray to the head detected two areas of impact on the calvaria, one on the right parietal bone and one on the occipital bone, with radiating

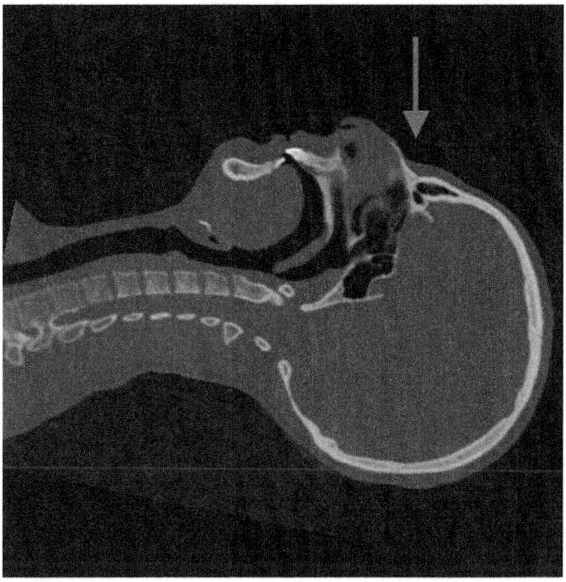

Figure 8.3 Nasal bones.

fractures originating from both areas (Fig. 8.4). Those anatomical locations were not consistent with the classical kicking act of bovines. The anatomical structure of their pelvis and lower limbs allows bovines to kick forward and out to the side, and usually produce fractures of the pelvis and lower limbs of the people around them. Furthermore, the same X-rays identified a detached bone fragment from the antero-inferior corner of the vertebral body of C3 (Fig. 8.5). The biomechanics of the vertebral body fracture suggest a violent hyperflexion of the head on the chest. Traditional radiography was essential to reconstruct the dynamics of the two blows to the victim's head, thus ruling out accidents and directing the investigation towards a homicide. The case remains unsolved.

Case 5 regarded the largely skeletonized body of an aged gentleman, whose identity was suspected and whose death was eventually filed as natural beyond reasonable doubt. A 2D full-body CT scan disclosed widespread osteoarthritis, a sternal metal surgical suture (Fig. 8.6A,B) and a spiral fracture of the left humerus (Fig. 8.7A,B). The sternal surgical suture matched the

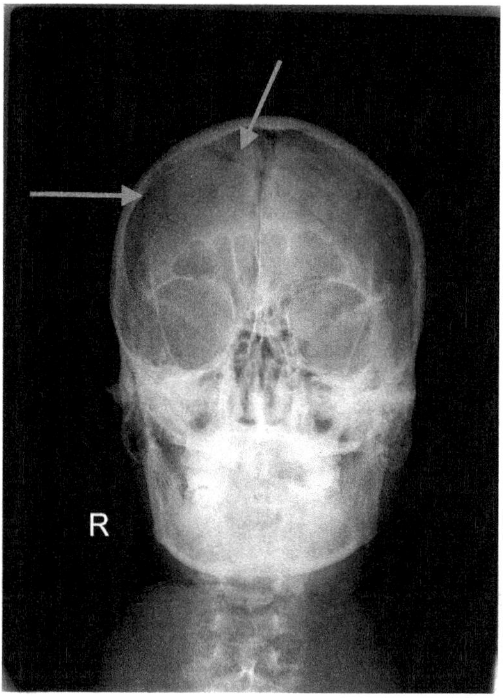

Figure 8.4 Radiating fractures on the calvaria.

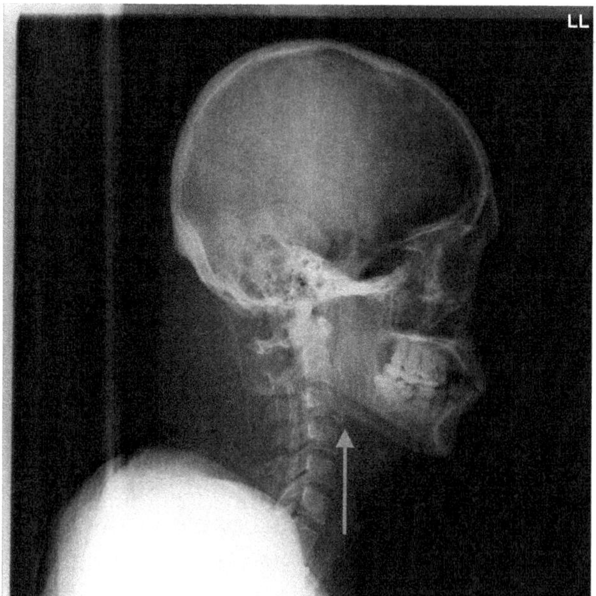

Figure 8.5 Fracture of the body of C3 with a detached bone fragment.

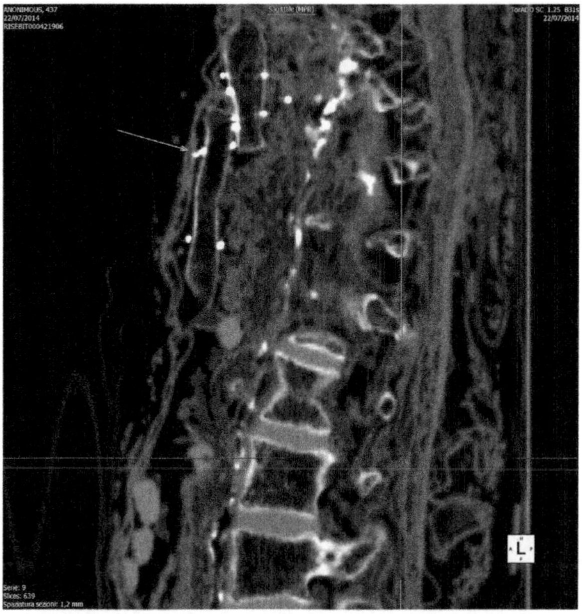

(A)

(B)

Figure 8.6 Sternal metal surgical suture, CT scan and autopsy.

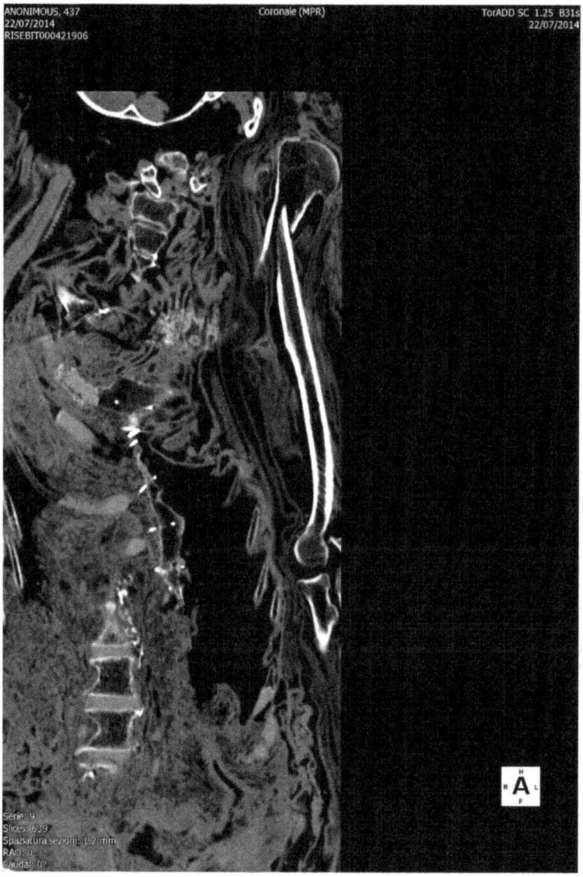

(A)

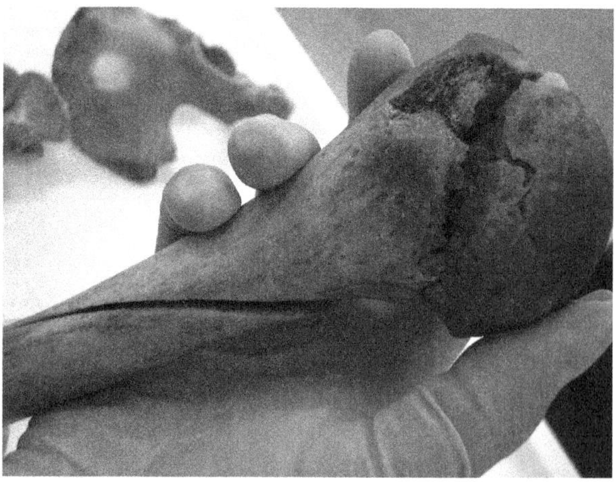

(B)

Figure 8.7 Spiral fracture of the left humerus, CT scan and autopsy.

case history of a cardiac pacemaker implant. The pacemaker was later recovered at the autopsy, and associated with the suspected identity by the matching of the production serial number. The humeral fracture, attributable to a perimortem event, shed a bit of light on the circumstances of death. The deceased had always been a keen hiker, and he was hiking alone at the time of his death, when he lost balance, most likely as a consequence of a sudden illness, and fractured his left humerus in the fall. His body was found in an isolated spot close to a camping site on the hills, where he was holidaying.

In our small case study, postmortem imaging was always carried out before the traditional autopsy, but achieving postmortem imaging after the autopsy can be justified in limited cases reported in the literature (Visentin, Pelletti, Dengo, De Matteis, & Montisci, 2017; Woźniak, Moskała, Konopka, Rzepecka-Woźniak, & Kluza, 2013).

References

Aalders, M. C., Adolphi, N. L., Daly, B., Davis, G. G., de Boer, H. H., Decker, S. J., ... Wozniak, K. (2017). Research in forensic radiology and imaging; Identifying the most important issues. *Journal of Forensic Radiology and Imaging*, *8*, 1–8. Available from https://doi.org/10.1016/j.jofri.2017.01.004.

Ahmad, M. U., Sharif, K. A., Qayyum, H., Ehsanullah, B., Balyasnikova, S., Wale, A., ... Athanasiou, T. (2017). Assessing the use of magnetic resonance imaging virtopsy as an alternative to autopsy: a systematic review and meta-analysis. *Postgraduate Medical Journal*, *93*(1105), 671–678. Available from https://doi.org/10.1136/postgradmedj-2017-134945.

Ampanozi, G., Gascho, D., Hatch, G., Schulze, C., Thali, M. J., & Ruder, T. D. (2014). What is unsought will go undetected – myocardial bridging on postmortem computed tomography. *Journal of Forensic Radiology and Imaging*, *2*(1), 5–8. Available from https://doi.org/10.1016/j.jofri.2013.11.010.

Baglivo, M., Winklhofer, S., Hatch, G. M., Ampanozi, G., Thali, M. J., & Ruder, T. D. (2013). The rise of forensic and post-mortem radiology—analysis of the literature between the year 2000 and 2011. *Journal of Forensic Radiology and Imaging*, *1*(1), 3–9. Available from https://doi.org/10.1016/j.jofri.2012.10.003.

Baier, W., Warnett, J. M., Payne, M., & Williams, M. A. (2018). Introducing 3D printed models as demonstrative evidence at criminal trials. *Journal of Forensic Sciences*, *63*(4), 1298–1302. Available from https://doi.org/10.1111/1556-4029.13700.

Bolliger, S. A., Thali, M. J., Ross, S., Buck, U., Naether, S., & Vock, P. (2007). Virtual autopsy using imaging: bridging radiologic and forensic sciences. A review of the Virtopsy and similar projects. *European radiology*, *18*(2), 273–282. Available from https://doi.org/10.1007/s00330-007-0737-4.

Brough, A. L., Morgan, B., & Rutty, G. N. (2015). The basics of disaster victim identification. *Journal of Forensic Radiology and Imaging*, *3*(1), 29–37. Available from https://doi.org/10.1016/j.jofri.2015.01.002.

Carew, R. M., & Errickson, D. (2019). Imaging in forensic science: five years on. *Journal of Forensic Radiology and Imaging*, *16*, 24–33. Available from https://doi.org/10.1016/j.jofri.2019.01.002.

Carew, R. M., & Errickson, D. (2020). An overview of 3D printing in forensic science: the tangible third-dimension. *Journal of Forensic Sciences*. Available from https://doi.org/10.1111/1556-4029.14442, *n/a*(n/a).

Charlier, P., Carlier, R., Roffi, F., Ezra, J., Chaillot, P. F., Duchat, F., ... de la Grandmaison, G. (2011). Postmortem abdominal CT: assessing normal cadaveric modifications and pathological processes. *European Journal of Radiology*, *81*(4), 639–647. Available from https://doi.org/10.1016/j.ejrad.2011.01.054.

Chatzaraki, V., Heimer, J., Thali, M., Dally, A., & Schweitzer, W. (2018). Role of PMCT as a triage tool between external inspection and full autopsy – Case series and review. *Journal of Forensic Radiology and Imaging*, *15*, 26–38. Available from https://doi.org/10.1016/j.jofri.2018.10.002.

Christe, A., Flach, P., Ross, S., Spendlove, D., Bolliger, S., Vock, P., & Thali, M. J. (2010). Clinical radiology and postmortem imaging (Virtopsy) are not the same: Specific and unspecific postmortem signs. *Legal Medicine*, *12*(5), 215–222. Available from https://doi.org/10.1016/j.legalmed.2010.05.005.

Cirielli, V., Cima, L., Bortolotti, F., Narayanasamy, M., Scarpelli, M., Danzi, O., ... Tagliaro, F. (2018). Virtual autopsy as a screening test before traditional autopsy: the verona experience on 25 Cases. *Journal of Pathology Informatics*, *9*(1). Available from https://doi.org/10.4103/jpi.jpi_23_18, 28-28.

Doyle, E., Márquez-Grant, N., Field, L., Holmes, T., Arthurs, O. J., van Rijn, R. R., ... Garamendi, P. M. (2019). Guidelines for best practice: Imaging for age estimation in the living. *Journal of Forensic Radiology and Imaging*, *16*, 38–49. Available from https://doi.org/10.1016/j.jofri.2019.02.001.

Ebert, L. C., Thali, M. J., & Ross, S. (2011). Getting in touch—3D printing in Forensic Imaging. *Forensic Science International*, *211*(1), e1–e6. Available from https://doi.org/10.1016/j.forsciint.2011.04.022.

Flach, P. M., Gascho, D., Schweitzer, W., Ruder, T. D., Berger, N., Ross, S. G., ... Ampanozi, G. (2014). Imaging in forensic radiology: an illustrated guide for postmortem computed tomography technique and protocols. *Forensic Science, Medicine, and Pathology*, *10*(4), 583–606. Available from https://doi.org/10.1007/s12024-014-9555-6.

Franckenberg, S., Flach, P. M., Gascho, D., Thali, M. J., & Ross, S. G. (2015). Postmortem computed tomography-angiography (PMCTA) in decomposed bodies – a feasibility study. *Journal of Forensic Radiology and Imaging*, *3*(4), 226–234. Available from https://doi.org/10.1016/j.jofri.2015.11.002.

Franckenberg, S., Kern, F., Vogt, M., Thali, M. J., & Flach, P. M. (2015). Fatal gunshot to a fox: The Virtopsy approach in a forensic veterinary case. *Journal of Forensic Radiology and Imaging*, *3*(1), 72–75. Available from https://doi.org/10.1016/j.jofri.2014.11.001.

Iino, M., & Aoki, Y. (2016). The use of radiology in the Japanese tsunami DVI process. *Journal of Forensic Radiology and Imaging*, *4*, 20–26. Available from https://doi.org/10.1016/j.jofri.2015.12.006.

Jackowski, C., Sonnenschein, M., Thali, M. J., Aghayev, E., von Allmen, G., Yen, K., … Vock, P. (2005). Virtopsy: postmortem minimally invasive angiography using cross section techniques--implementation and preliminary results. *Journal of Forensic Sciences*, *50*(5), 1175. Retrieved from http://murdoch.summon.serialssolutions.com/2.0.0/link/0/eLvHCXMwtV1JS8NAFB6qXgQR913mHiKZJpk0ggcRRc8uV5nOosUmmDV0U_fW-2ZJQVPTgJYQMCWTe17ek3_seQnH3JArnfAJgh3OSyUjkScRYX8mIcxFJHU-gphZencHQVDsdPyx0jrr6X4aHa2B63Uj7B-PXD4ULcA4QgCOAAI6_gsHDYDwdVROj61SNJtPCkGsDrShSsOFQd_29MkNhZ-XTwOlXBzPbi6sjaDCRdpp4rfY6CcNB4WnnU09nrsZyaCaEjd8DKOFnQysR9UXiC2myZs3zwEXfhsTI-MvozQ3StqoHLfDeakpOCcW4G89pBRAaYguzjd6uD6D5u-v86Zm9w7Zpp1-4G_xnjrTmcbXbDgixI6tPpPPWKdUFcN5251bH1sE2bflmLUraDhqw8VVhzE4oeLWu7dz_eXVOm7te0jrthRjw6Zksw_vbBbQEaWFmCpmbqzozoIQSr16vX0Ur1ronzFU1Jru5W0Orzjr43AJoHXVkuYFW7DddbFvVNtGHB9MpbqCEayhhDyXcghI2UMIGSthBCX8PJbhV4BaUsIPSFrq_ury7uA7d7I4QEsYsCWnMZJZqqSalpMpTM4mV93OVi0QwlREtY5TEEDBUwqBooEx0k5wxwSDgcZp2t9FiOSrlLsIxiaXsqx7lcZRIqvIs7vWUgMSaikhIsod27NY9Vlag5dFv6v63KwdouQHZIVpS8HOXR_UMsWNjt09f3Ie8.

Klein, W. M., Kunz, T., Hermans, K., Bayat, A. R., & Koopmanschap, D. H. J. L. M. (2016). The common pattern of postmortem changes on whole body CT scans. *Journal of Forensic Radiology and Imaging*, *4*, 47–52. Available from https://doi.org/10.1016/j.jofri.2015.11.006.

Le Garff, E., Mesli, V., Delannoy, Y., Colard, T., Demondion, X., Becart, A., & Hedouin, V. (2017). Technical note: early post-mortem changes of human bone in taphonomy with μCT. *International Journal of Legal Medicine*, *131*(3), 761–770. Available from https://doi.org/10.1007/s00414-016-1509-y.

Obertová, Z., Leipner, A., Messina, C., Vanzulli, A., Fliss, B., Cattaneo, C., & Sconfienza, L. M. (2019). Postmortem imaging of perimortem skeletal trauma. *Forensic Science International*, *302*, 109921. Available from https://doi.org/10.1016/j.forsciint.2019.109921.

Oesterhelweg, L., Bolliger, S. A., Thali, M. J., & Ross, S. (2009). Virtopsy: postmortem imaging of laryngeal foreign bodies. *Archives of Pathology & Laboratory Medicine*, *133*(5), 806. Retrieved from http://murdoch.summon.serialssolutions.com/2.0.0/link/0/eLvHCXMwpV1LT8JAEJ4gJMaL7wei2JsnpN3u0tbEmEpo5CAYo8Zbs213CYm0DZQD_96dtoBwMvGySdNJ2-zO49vuzDcAJrnTW1s-QXJLmGbU4SZhnHPkFO9QxkPOFV4iMliyM-RpqhXoLktj8uR3dJW50-ZpOmtHSdh2FXA2kDCItd3hoPf4q5nG_KHk1t6Bmgr2Fmp63x2uiXhJUYvFqNkiBsaUbVe8BTDzQOMdwPf670qRYbLF4b3J4vjPjz-E_RKQam6hQUdQEfEx7L6UR-4nYH-Op1mSzhb3WprMskmenKuNJ3l3Iy2RmtoaL-KRwpuaLNp8akGCqYmn8OH13rvPrbLdQmtkKNiIRTrCNAJObWpSbI1LAkeElHJGHCpZJGwaIsGZuq8MWXBdSeoRMtoTYiHh5xlU4yQWF6CZ-QiehzexIRhHVBW6qIhk61LEDQyqIVYcbnBe_qPVcGZm_npo63OYSaGbZVClKW-S2gno-EVRuSjeXK-aX9zXwVkHWGu586nBeL6acFe4dvOAqzOMy-_PMbGrBXnCFhmuMVVLPpXFyv-k01Ycf6sppQe-oNXt_UVa_vqdFzu81c83Acej_KR-Q9.

Ruder, T. D., Thali, Y. A., Rashid, S. N. A., Mund, M. T., Thali, M. J., Hatch, G. M., … Ampanozi, G. (2016). Validation of post mortem dental CT for disaster victim identification. *Journal of Forensic Radiology and Imaging*, *5*, 25–30. Available from https://doi.org/10.1016/j.jofri.2016.01.006.

Schweitzer, W., Spycher, I., Winklhofer, S., Thali, M. J., Ruder, T. D., Ampanozi, G., … Ross, S. G. (2013). Assessment of laryngeal tube placement on post mortem computed tomography scans. *Journal of Forensic Radiology and Imaging*, *1*(3), 119–123. Available from https://doi.org/10.1016/j.jofri.2013.04.001.

Simmons-Ehrhardt, T. L., Ehrhardt, C. J., & Monson, K. L. (2019). Evaluation of the suitability of cranial measurements obtained from surface-rendered CT scans of living people for estimating sex and ancestry. *Journal of Forensic Radiology and Imaging*, *19*, 100338. Available from https://doi.org/10.1016/j.jofri.2019.100338.

Tangmose, S., Jensen, K. E., & Lynnerup, N. (2013). Comparative study on developmental stages of the clavicle by postmortem MRI and CT imaging. *Journal of Forensic Radiology and Imaging*, *1*(3), 102–106. Available from https://doi.org/10.1016/j.jofri.2013.05.008.

Thali, M. J., Jackowski, C., Oesterhelweg, L., Ross, S. G., & Dirnhofer, R. (2007). VIRTOPSY – The Swiss virtual autopsy approach. *Legal Medicine*, *9*(2), 100–104. Available from https://doi.org/10.1016/j.legalmed.2006.11.011.

Thali, M. J., Schweitzer, W., Yen, K., Vock, P., Ozdoba, C., Spielvogel, E., & Dirnhofer, R. (2003). New horizons in forensic radiology: the 60-second digital autopsy-full-body examination of a gunshot victim by multislice computed tomography. *The American Journal of Forensic Medicine and Pathology*, *24*(1), 22. Retrieved from http://murdoch.summon.serialssolutions.com/2.0.0/link/0/eLvHCXMwtV1Lb9NAEF6lVEKVEIJCgfLQ3C1XfsR2WqkHhKjgwImUHqv1PmpXjR0lDm36H_jPnX3a-DUKUAxcr8ipOsvNldmbnm28JSZODKNzwCTShEwwOssNI5Lmup5UTGquDbjN-eTETi1Bk0TXU0cqKLG9TV_2V4vIemV420_2B8_1C8ga8RAnhFEOD1QTBQ_MWqXdS3ljGOMaqirLNgQbntVLHMjjwKlyo75gGvL9RRIgFdde18uQ7VFn1YtnwdiBu-qqDMuyqTBxapZVm0X_FSdJTMVy2qGIgavTGi6-kpFtF07GypjX_YI9QWjgYKF_4qu7m_EDGhX3SsBTCtqWrst839Q4GLVtai7W4PGs_ZK9jvDjaOQLGr_t_hh14Seq-y2QdKeB-Z2Rg-19qYp8gjnzVNMkA0F1Ll707J9D9bWdyfDJQUnfz7ToIgx5cO8MP376IZytx9SKu4znLHuWDTh6fctso1BY6HTnK8nPm5Ix5oh63-I0rO1T9jIeXTsM31G31GntqkBT4aeD0nI9HsksffrHl2yROz-Qump-0F-YWoA4c6qBtwJgWPuiNAzIHHHFjMwW-YgwHmoJVAwWIODOagXEOPOXCYgx5zL8npyefppy-hPfcjZBiMjkOe5aWMKLqGmCvZU5nxfMwKhqktrj4lxsA8yXHhKKlUx2xJ9CuJiFmWSxrzWIyTPfKoaRvxmkBRpCylSoZUSfHxiHI5YSl-ChcxvkW8Ia_MxJ7PjbjLuZvy_T-OvCU7PQDfkW2JrkK89-ePfdBWvQNn7pl3.

Tschui, J., Jackowski, C., Schwendener, N., Schyma, C., & Zech, W. D. (2016). Postmortem CT and MR brain imaging of putrefied corpses. *International Journal of Legal Medicine*, *130*(4), 1061–1068. Available from https://doi.org/10.1007/s00414-016-1385-5.

van Kan, R. A. T., Haest, I. I. H., Lahaye, M. J., & Hofman, P. A. M. (2017). The diagnostic value of forensic imaging in fatal gunshot incidents: a review of literature. *Journal of Forensic Radiology and Imaging*, *10*, 9–14. Available from https://doi.org/10.1016/j.jofri.2017.07.003.

Visentin, S., Pelletti, G., Dengo, C., De Matteis, M., & Montisci, M. (2017). Post-autopsy computed tomography. Pros and cons in a firearm death. *Forensic Science International*, *276*, e16–e19. Available from https://doi.org/10.1016/j.forsciint.2017.04.017.

Western, A. G., & Bekvalac, J. J. (2017). Hyperostosis frontalis interna in female historic skeletal populations: age, sex hormones and the impact of industrialization. *American Journal of Physical Anthropology, 162*(3), 501–515. Available from https://doi.org/10.1002/ajpa.23133.

Woźniak, K., Moskała, A., Konopka, T., Rzepecka-Woźniak, E., & Kluza, P. (2013). PMCT in cases of forensic examination of previously autopsied corpses. *Journal of Forensic Radiology and Imaging, 1*(2), 79. Available from https://doi.org/10.1016/j.jofri.2013.03.036.

INDEX

Note: Page numbers followed by "*f*" and "*t*" refer to figures and tables, respectively.

9780128242940